The Craving Mind

THE CRAVING MIND

FROM CIGARETTES TO SMARTPHONES TO LOVE—WHY WE GET HOOKED AND HOW WE CAN BREAK BAD HABITS

● ● ●

JUDSON BREWER

FOREWORD BY JON KABAT-ZINN

Yale

UNIVERSITY PRESS

New Haven and London

The information and suggestions contained in this book are not intended to replace the services of your physician or caregiver. Because each person and each medical situation is unique, you should consult your own physician to get answers to your personal questions, to evaluate any symptoms you may have, or to receive suggestions for appropriate medications.

The author has attempted to make this book as accurate and up to date as possible, but it may nevertheless contain errors, omissions, or material that is out of date at the time you read it. Neither the author nor the publisher has any legal responsibility or liability for errors, omissions, out-of-date material, or the reader's application of the medical information or advice contained in this book.

Published with assistance from the Louis Stern Memorial Fund.

Yale University Press books may be purchased in quantity for educational, business, or promotional use. For information, please e-mail sales.press@ yale.edu (U.S. office) or sales@yaleup.co.uk (U.K. office).

Printed in the United States of America.

Library of Congress Control Number: 2016953453
ISBN 978-0-300-22324-8 (hardcover : alk. paper)
ISBN 978-0-300-23436-7 (pbk.)

A catalogue record for this book is available from the British Library.

10 9 8 7 6

For all those who suffer

Contents

The Craving Mind

Jon Kabat-Zinn

It is an incontrovertible fact, although it usually goes unrecognized and unappreciated, that right inside each one of our heads, underneath the encompassing vault of the cranium and weighing in at around three pounds (approximately two percent of the body's weight), is found the most complex organization of matter in the known-by-us universe, namely the human brain. That makes us rather remarkable in terms of what we are capable of. The miracle of being human can be readily seen everywhere once you train your eye and your heart to look. It transcends and embraces all the pain and suffering that comes with the human condition, and that we so often cause ourselves and one another by ignoring who and what we really are. It is so easy to fall into ruts, bad habits, even depression, thirsting for what we feel we need to complete ourselves, what we might need to feel at home in our own skin, truly at peace in our life, even if just for a brief moment, or an hour or a day. All the while, ironically, we are missing the fact that we are actually conspiring to make ourselves slaves to an illusion, to the compulsive longing to complete ourselves when, in fact, we are already complete, already whole. But somehow, we momentarily forget this, or never remember it, or perhaps we feel so wounded that we cannot even entertain the possibility of our own essential completeness without a lot of support, and a method, a path to reclaim that wholeness (the root meaning of the words "health" and "healing") and our beauty. This book provides just such a path, well demarcated and expertly guided by the author. You are now at the trailhead, a perfect place to begin the adventure of reclaiming the full dimensionality of your being and learning to embody your wholeness in the face of the undermining addictiveness of the craving mind.

Until quite recently, the extent of the brain's complex structures, networks, and functions, its uncanny plasticity, and its versatility as a multidimensional self-organizing learning matrix—a result of billions of years of evolution that is continuing to evolve surprisingly rapidly both biologically and culturally in our time—was not fully appreciated even by scientists. Now, given recent advances in neuroscience and technology, we stand in awe of the brain's architecture and its seemingly boundless repertoire of capacities and functions, to say nothing of its totally mysterious property of sentience. In contemplating it, we swallow hard at the immensity of our human inheritance and at the challenges we might live up to in the relatively short period of time each of us has between birth and death, were we to recognize the full extent of that inheritance and what it might portend in terms of being more fully awake, more fully aware, more fully embodied, more fully connected, freer from the confines of our unhealthy and imprisoning habits, in sum, more fully who and what we actually are, given the truly miraculous nature of this mysterious emergence and its capacities and possibilities.

Think of it—and, of course, marvel that you can think at all, of anything—your own brain is comprised of approximately eighty-six billion individual nerve cells (by latest measure), called neurons, with millions of them extending themselves into every domain within the body, our eyes and ears, nose, tongue, skin, and, via the spinal cord and autonomic nervous system, to virtually every location and organ in the body.[1] Those eighty-six billion neurons in the brain have at least that many partner cells, called glial cells, whose functions are not well understood but are thought to at least in part support the neurons and keep them healthy and happy, although there is the suspicion that they may be doing much, much more. The neurons themselves are organized in many highly specific and specialized ways into circuits within the larger differentiated regions of the brain, the cortex,[2] the midbrain, the cerebellum, the brain stem, and in the various loci, or "nuclei," which include unique structures such as the thalamus, the hypothalamus, the hippocampus, the amygdala, and so forth that subtend and integrate so many of the functions of the organism. These functions include movement and locomotion, approach-avoidance behaviors, learning and memory, emotion and cognition and their continual regulation, the sensing of the outer world, and the sensing of the body itself through various "maps" of the body located in different regions of the cortex, the "reading" of the emotions and mind states of others, feeling empathy and compassion for others, as well as, of course, all aspects of the aforementioned sentience, the very essence of what makes us human, consciousness itself.

Each of those eighty-six billion neurons has about ten thousand synapses, so there are hundreds of trillions of synaptic connections between neurons in the brain, a virtually infinite and continually changing web of networks for adapting to ever-changing circumstances and complexities, and in particular, for learning, so as to optimize our chances of survival and our individual and collective well-being. These circuits are continually remaking themselves as a function of what we do or don't do, what we encounter, and how we choose to relate to it. The very connectivity of our brain seems to be shaped and enhanced as a function of what we pursue, enact, recognize, and embody.

Our habits, our actions, our behaviors, and our very thoughts drive, reinforce, and ultimately consolidate what is called functional connectivity in the brain, the linking up of different areas to make essential connections, to make things possible that weren't before. That is what learning does. It turns out, it can happen very fast if you are paying attention in a particular way, using the mindfulness compass described in this book. Or if we don't give our attention to unwanted or aversive circumstances, that inattention just deepens the habitual ruts in the mind that are carved out by craving and our various life-constraining addictions, small and large, leading to endless rounds of reactivity and suffering. So the stakes are quite high for each of us.

Given the intimacy of this infinitude of complexity and capacity lying within our own heads—now that neuroscience has revealed it and we realize that more and more fascinating dimensions of the brain continue to be discovered every day—we are undeniably challenged to make use of what is known so far to better understand our own lives and how we live them so as to put this vast repertoire to work for us in the service of health, happiness, creativity, imagination, and, ultimately, deep well-being, not merely for ourselves, but for others as well, those with whom we share our lives and our planet.

And with this inheritance of exquisitely organized complexity and beauty on so many levels lying within us, it staggers the mind to realize—oh, I neglected to mention that out of all this, apparently, comes a sense of self and a sense of that "self" having a mind!—it staggers the mind to realize that we still suffer, we get depressed, we get anxious, we harm others as well as ourselves, and ironically, fall easily into relatively unconscious habit patterns to soothe ourselves, habits that can be highly destructive of the very well-being we are yearning for.

And much of this suffering, this out-of-jointness, comes from feeling as if something is still missing even though we have it all and are undeniably miraculous beings, geniuses really, and gifted beyond compare with possibilities for learning, growing, healing, and transformation across the life span. How are we to understand this? Why do we feel so empty, so in need of continual gratification and the incessant and immediate satisfying of our desires? When all is said and done, *what,* in actuality, are we craving? And *why* are we craving it? And when you come right down to it, *who* is it who is actually craving anyway? Who owns your brain? Who is in charge? Who suffers as a consequence? Who might make things right?

These questions are addressed and answered admirably in this compelling book by Judson Brewer, director of the Therapeutic Neuroscience Laboratory at the Center for Mindfulness in Medicine, Health Care, and Society at the University of Massachusetts Medical School. As a psychiatrist with a long-standing clinical practice in the field of addiction psychiatry, Jud has developed deep insight into the challenges of pervasive addictions of all kinds, and the downstream disorders and diseases and the pain and suffering that they ultimately cause us, all stemming from the mind-state of craving, a tendency we all share to one degree or another, being human, and that we also either ignore wholesale when it suits us or, in other instances, perhaps feel powerless to deal with—our own innate agency and transformative potential seemingly out of reach or even unrecognized.

In parallel with his trajectory within mainstream addiction psychiatry, Jud has been a long-term and highly devoted practitioner of mindfulness meditation, as well as a serious student of the classical Buddhist teachings, traditions, and sources that mindfulness meditation practices are based on. Delineated in exquisite and compelling detail thousands of years before it was recognized by Western psychology, craving plays a fundamental and pivotal role in the genesis of suffering and unhappiness in Buddhist psychology, as you will soon see.

What Jud has done in his clinical and laboratory work, and now in this book, is to bring those two universes of understanding of the mind in general, and of its addictive tendencies in particular, together to inform each other and to show us how simple mindfulness practices have the potential, both in the moment and over time, to actually release and thereby free us from cravings of all kind, including, ultimately, the craving to protect a very limited sense of self that may have outgrown its usefulness, and that may simultaneously be missing the point that the "you" who is craving something is only a small part of the much larger "you" who knows that craving is arising and driving your behavior in one unfortunate way or another, and who also knows the sorry long-term consequences of that addictive patterning.

From the Western psychology side, we are introduced to B. F. Skinner's theory of operant conditioning and its explanatory framework for understanding human behavior. This perspective, while useful in some contexts, is also fraught with problematic aspects and severe limitations, being so behaviorist in orientation that it leaves no meaningful role for cognitive processes, never mind awareness itself. What is more, it is so tied to the admittedly powerful explanatory notion of *reward* that it typically ignores, or even denies outright, the equally powerful mysteries of agency, cognition, and selflessness. These human capacities transcend and obviate reward in the ways that notion is commonly understood from Skinner's classical animal studies and those of others. Some experiences, like the embodied, uncontrived comfort of knowing who you are, or at least investigating that domain with an open mind and heart, may be intrinsically and profoundly gratifying, and orthogonal to the conditioning of the typically externally oriented Skinnerian reward paradigm.

To transcend the limitations of the operant conditioning perspective of behaviorism, Jud introduces us to the Buddhist framework within which mindfulness as a meditative discipline and practice evolved and flourished over millennia in Asian cultures, and to its systematic and very practical approach —grounded in the framework of the central Buddhist teachings on "dependent origination"—to learning how we can liberate ourselves from the dominance and sometimes tyranny of our own craving mind, first and foremost by paradoxically cultivating intimacy with it. And this all hinges on recognizing over and over again how tightly bound up we are in our own seemingly endless self-referencing, and on whether we can simply be aware of it without judging ourselves harshly and can cultivate other, more intentional options for *responding* mindfully rather than *reacting* mindlessly in those very moments when craving arises.

Self-referencing is a critical piece here. Recent work has shown that when people are asked to do nothing (in an fMRI scanner while their brain activity is being measured), they default to mind wandering, and much of those wandering thoughts take the form of an ongoing narrative about oneself, "the story of me," we could say: my future, my past, my successes, my failures, and so forth. What is seen in the brain scans is that a large midline region in the cortex starts lighting up, that is, shows a major increase in neural activity—even though you are being asked to do nothing inside the scanner. This region has been termed the default mode network (DMN), for obvious reasons. Sometimes it is also called the narrative network, because when we just let the mind do what it does, so much of it is caught up in the narrative about oneself, an aspect of our own mind that we are often completely unaware of unless we have had some training in mindfulness.

Work at the University of Toronto[3] showed that eight weeks of mindfulness training in the form of Mindfulness-Based Stress Reduction (MBSR) resulted in reduced activity in the narrative network, and in increased activity in a more lateral network of the cortex that is associated with present-moment awareness, experientially outside of time, and lacking any narrative at all. The researchers in this study refer to this neural circuitry as the experiential network. These findings are highly consonant with Jud's pioneering work on the default mode network with meditation, in both novice meditators and in those with many years of intensive practice and training.

Jud and his colleagues have developed novel neuroscientific technologies and methods that allow both Western psychological and classical meditative perspectives to be brought into the laboratory to investigate what is going on in the brain *in real time* while a person is meditating. As you will see, this is done by giving his experimental subjects direct visual feedback (and insight) into what is going on in their own brains moment by moment by moment in a particular region of the DMN known as the posterior cingulate cortex (PCC), a domain which seems to quiet down (diminish its electrical activity) during meditation under certain circumstances—specifically, when the subject gives up trying to get anywhere or make anything happen other than be present.

Mindfulness as both a formal meditation practice and as a way of living has two interacting aspects, an *instrumental* dimension and a *non-instrumental* dimension. The instrumental dimension involves learning the practices and experiencing the benefits (Jud would say "rewards") of such practices, much as what happens when one undertakes any kind of ongoing learning process, like driving a car or playing a musical instrument. With continued practice, we get better and better at the task, in this case, the challenge of being present and aware of what our own mind is up to, especially when it is caught up in subtle and not so subtle craving, and then perhaps learning how to not be so easily caught by those mental energies and habit patterns.

The non-instrumental dimension, a true complement to the instrumental dimension of mindfulness practice and absolutely essential to its cultivation and to freeing ourselves from craving-associated mind states, thoughts, and emotions, is that there is, at the very same time—and this is very hard to take in or talk about, which is why the phenomenon of *flow* plays such a large role in this book—no place to go, nothing to do, no special state to attain, and, ultimately, no one (in the conventional sense of a "you" or a "me") to attain it.

Both of these dimensions of mindfulness are simultaneously true. Yes, you do need to practice, but if you try too hard or strive for some desired end point and its attendant reward, then you are simply shifting the craving to a new object or a new goal or a new attachment and a new or merely upgraded or revised "story of me." Inside this tension between the instrumental and the non-instrumental lies the true extinguishing of craving,[4] and of the "mis-taken" perceptions of yourself that the craving habit is grounded in. Jud's real-time neurofeedback studies of activity changes in the PCC during meditation practice, vividly showing what happened in the PCC when his subjects got caught up in *trying* to bring about an effect, and what happened when they got excited because they *did*, are dramatic demonstrations of the powerful effects within the brain of non-doing, non-striving, and getting out of your own way in order to be fully present and emotionally equanimous. These studies are a remarkable contribution to our understanding of different meditative practices, of the various mind states that can arise during formal or informal meditation practices, and their potential relationship to the vast, open, thought-free spaciousness of awareness itself.

This book and the work it is based on, which is described in a user-friendly prose that makes the complex science easy to grasp, offer us a radically new perspective on learning, on breaking habits of mind not by force or through the application of will power or the clutching for a momentary and fleeting reward, but by truly inhabiting the domain of being, by becoming intimate with the space of pure awareness itself, and by discovering how available it is right in this timeless moment we call now. Indeed, as Henry David Thoreau knew and described in great detail in *Walden,* there is no other moment in which wakeful presence and equanimity are to be located. And nothing has to happen other than to learn how to rest in awareness and be the knowing (and at times, the not-knowing) that "your" awareness already is and that "you" already have. Habits dissolve in the face of this inhabiting of the space of awareness. But the irony is that it is a non-trivial undertaking, this non-doing. It is the adventure of a lifetime, yet it requires a significant investment of effort— paradoxically, the effort of no-effort, and the knowing of not- knowing—particularly in regard to the process of "selfing," the inveterate and usually unrecognized generating of the story of me.

As noted, part of the Western perspective on addiction stems from the work of B. F. Skinner, the father of operant conditioning. In this regard, Jud quotes from Skinner's novel, *Walden Two,* and its all- too-prescient foreseeing of social engineering in our digitally inter- connected world. Happily, however, the highly behavioristic reward- based Skinnerian perspective on addiction is balanced out here by a transcendent wisdom perspective that has much more in common with the original *Walden,* what we could call *"Walden One."* Jud does this not by citing Thoreau, but by describing the phenomenon of flow experiences and their physiology and psychology, based on the pioneering work of the contemporary Hungarian psychologist Mihály Csíkszentmihályi, and by pointing to the non-duality that lies at the heart of the Buddhist teachings of selflessness and emptiness, non-grasping, non-clinging, and non-craving. These domains and insights were all clearly seen and beautifully articulated by T. S. Eliot in his own transcendent poetic affirmations and insights in his culminating work, *Four Quartets,* from which Jud quotes incisively.

As you will learn, our habits of craving seem to be the root cause of so much of our suffering, both large and small. We may indeed be driven by and to distraction, especially with the addictiveness of our digital technologies and speed-driven lifestyles. But the good news is, once we know this up close and personal, there is so much we can do to free ourselves from that suffering and live much more satisfying, healthy, original, ethical, and truly productive lives.

Jud walks us through all of this in a masterful, personal, friendly, humorous, and erudite way. Moreover, consistent with our times, he and his colleagues have developed, and he describes them here, highly sophisticated smartphone apps to support your mindfulness practice, especially if you are coming to it in part to quit smoking or to change your eating habits.

There is no better time than now to take up the practices offered in this book and make use of them to transform your life and free yourself from the kinds of forces that always have us missing or discounting the fullness and beauty of this moment, and of our wholeness now, as we try to fill imaginary holes of dissatisfaction and longing that feel so real and yet cannot be satisfied by further cycles of craving and succumbing to whatever gives us transient relief. Still, if you fall into delusion—as we all do from time to time, and as Jud describes he did in a major way with his own elaborate infatuation-based engagement scenario—and you fail to recognize it, as he disarmingly recounts so candidly—sooner or later you may realize that there is always the opportunity to wake up and recognize the cost of craving and the imprisoning effects of our addictions, and begin again.

May navigating this trail of mindfulness you are about to embark on lead you ever closer to your own heart and your own authenticity, and toward freedom from the incessant grip of the craving mind.

Jon Kabat-Zinn

Notes

1. James Randerson, "How Many Neurons Make a Human Brain?" *Guardian*, February 28, 2012, https://www.theguardian.com/science/blog/2012/feb/28/how-many-neurons-human-brain; Bradley Voytek, "Are There Really as Many Neurons in the Human Brain as Stars in the Milky Way?" Scitable, May 20, 2013, www.nature.com/scitable/blog/brain-metrics/are_there_really_as_many.

2. Ninety-seven more uniquely distinguishable regions of the cerebral cortex alone, never before recognized, were just reported in the journal *Nature* as I write this, in addition to the eighty-two already known.

3. Norman A. S. Farb, Zindel V. Segal, Helen Mayberg, et al., "Attending to the Present: Mindfulness Meditation Reveals Distinct Neural Modes of Self-Reference," *Social Cognitive and Affective Neuroscience* 2, no. 4 (2007): 313–22. doi:10.1093/scan/nsm030.

4. "Extinguished," as in a fire being put out, is the literal meaning of "nirvana" in Pali, the original language of the Buddha.

Preface

I started having gastrointestinal "issues" during my senior year of college. Bloating, cramping, gas, and frequent bowel movements made me look constantly for bathrooms that were close at hand. I even changed my daily running route so that I could get to a bathroom quickly if nature called. Clever me, I self-diagnosed my issues as a bacterial infection caused by the parasite *Giardia lamblia,* since it causes somewhat similar symptoms. I figured that it made logical sense: I had spent a lot of time leading backpacking trips throughout college, and a common cause of giardiasis is improper purification of drinking water, which might have occurred while camping.

When I went to see the doctor at the student health center, I shared my diagnosis with him. He parried, "Are you stressed?" I remember saying something like, "No way! I run, I eat healthy food, I play in the orchestra. There is no way I can be stressed—all this healthy stuff that I'm doing is supposed to keep me from getting stressed!" He smiled, gave me the antibiotic that treats giardiasis— and my symptoms didn't improve.

It was only later that I learned that I had presented the classic symptoms of irritable bowel syndrome (IBS), a symptom-based diagnosis with "no known organic [that is, physical] cause." In other words, I had a physical illness caused by my head. I might have found this advice offensive—"get right in the head and you'll be fine"—but a family life event changed my mind.

My future sister-in-law was in the throes of planning a double event—a blowout New Year's Eve party that would also serve as her wedding reception. The following day—and not because of too much champagne—she got very sick right at the beginning of her honeymoon. It got me thinking that there might be something to this mind-body connection. While that kind of reasoning is mostly respected today, several decades ago it fell into the realm of holding hands and singing "Kumbaya." That wasn't me. I was an organic chemistry major studying the molecules of life—far from New Age snake oil. After the wedding, I became fascinated by the simple question, why do we get sick when we are stressed?

And with this, my life path changed.

That was the question I took to medical school. After graduating from Princeton, I started a joint MD-PhD program at Washington University in St. Louis. These programs are a great way to meld medicine and science—take real-world problems that doctors see every day, study them in the lab, and come up with ways to improve care. My plan was to figure out how stress affects our immune systems and can lead to such things as my sister-in-law getting sick just after her big day. I joined the lab of Louis Muglia, who was an expert in both endocrinology and neuroscience. We hit it off right away, since we shared the same passion for understanding how stress makes us sick. I got down to work, manipulating stress hormone gene expression in mice to see what happened to their immune systems. And we (along with many other scientists) discovered many fascinating things.

Yet I entered medical school still stressed out. In addition to the IBS—which, thankfully, had improved—I was having trouble sleeping, for the first time in my life. Why? Just before starting school, I had broken up with my fiancée, my college sweetheart of several years, with whom I had already set a long-term life plan. The breakup was not part of the plan.

So here I was, about to start an important new phase of my life, insomnia ridden and single. Jon Kabat-Zinn's *Full Catastrophe Living: Using the Wisdom of Your Body and Mind to Face Stress, Pain, and Illness* (1990) somehow fell into my lap. Feeling as though I could relate to the "full catastrophe" part of the title, I dove in and started meditating on my first day of medical school. Exactly twenty years later, I now look back and see that my encounter with this book was one of the most important events in my life. Reading *Full Catastrophe* changed the entire trajectory of what I was doing, who I was, and who I still am becoming.

Being the "go big or go home" kind of person that I was at the time, I dove into meditation practice with the same fervor with which I had approached other things in life. I meditated every morning. I meditated during boring medical school lectures. I started attending meditation retreats. I began studying with a meditation teacher. I started discovering where my stress was coming from and how I was contributing to it. I began to see connections between early Buddhist teachings and modern scientific discoveries. I started to get a glimpse into how my mind worked.

Eight years later, when I finished my MD-PhD program, I chose to train as a psychiatrist—not because of the pay (psychiatrists are among the lowest paid of all physicians) or reputation (Hollywood portrays shrinks as either ineffectual charlatans or manipulative Svengalis), but because I was seeing clear connections between ancient and current psychological models of behavior, especially addiction. Halfway through my psychiatry training, I shifted my research emphasis from molecular biology and immunology to mindfulness: how it affects the brain and how it can help improve psychiatric conditions.

The past twenty years have been full of fascinating personal, clinical, and scientific explorations. For the first decade, I never considered applying my mindfulness practice clinically or scientifically. I simply practiced. And practiced. My personal exploration later provided the critical foundation for my work as both a psychiatrist and a scientist. When I trained in psychiatry, the connections began flowing naturally between what I had learned conceptually and what I had gained experientially from mindfulness practice. I saw a clear impact on my patient care, both when I was and when I wasn't being mindful. When sleep deprived after an overnight call at the hospital, I could see clearly that I was more likely to snap at my teammates, and my mindfulness practice helped me hold back from doing this. When I was truly present for my patients, mindfulness helped me not jump to diagnostic conclusions or make assumptions, and fostered a deeper interpersonal connection as well.

Also, the scientific part of my mind was fascinated by my personal and clinical observations. How did paying attention help me change my ingrained habits? How was it helping me connect with my patients? I began designing basic scientific and clinical studies to explore what happens in our brains when we are mindful, and how these insights can be translated into improving the lives of patients. From those results, I was able to begin optimizing treatment and delivery tools for the evidence-based trainings that we were developing, such as smoking cessation and stress or emotional eating.

My observations from scientific experiments, clinical encounters with patients, and my own mind have come together in ways that have helped me understand the world with much greater clarity. What once seemed random in how people behaved in studies and in my clinic, and even in how my mind operated, has become more orderly and predictable. This realization goes to the very heart of scientific discovery: being able to reproduce observations and predict results based on a set of rules or hypotheses.

My work has converged on a relatively simple principle based on an evolutionarily conserved learning process that was set up to help our ancestors survive. In a sense, this learning process has been co-opted to reinforce a wide breadth of behaviors, including day-dreaming, distraction, stress, and addiction.

As this principle started to gel in my mind, my scientific predictions improved, and I was able to empathize with and help my patients more. In addition, I became more focused, less stressed, and more engaged with the world around me. And as I began sharing some of these insights with my patients, my students, and the general public, I received feedback from them: they hadn't seen the link between these basic psychological and neurobiological principles and how they could apply them personally. Again and again, they told me that learning things this way—through mindfulness, stepping back and observing our own actions—helped the world make more sense to them. They were relating to themselves and the world differently. They were learning to make sustainable behavior changes. Their lives were improving. And they wanted me to write all this down in a way that was accessible so that they could see how everything fit together, and could continue to learn.

This book applies current—and emerging—scientific knowledge to everyday and clinical examples. It lays out a number of cases in which this evolutionarily beneficial learning process has gone awry or been hijacked by modern culture (including technology); its overall aim is to help us understand the origins of our diverse behaviors, from things as trivial as being distracted by our phones to experiences as meaningful as falling in love. In medicine, diagnosis is the first and most critical step. Building on this idea and following up on what I have learned in professional and personal practice, I outline simple, pragmatic ways to target these core mechanisms, methods that we all can apply to our everyday lives, whether to step out of our addictive habits, reduce stress, or simply live a fuller life.

Introduction

The Origin of Species

If I were your boss and you told me I had the brain of a sea slug, would I fire you for insulting me, or would I promote you to head of marketing for demonstrating that you *really* understood how humans think and behave?

What if I said that regardless of your beliefs about how humans came to be, one thing that has been demonstrated over and over is that human learning is very much like that of sea slugs—which have only twenty thousand neurons? And what if I pressed on to suggest that our learning patterns even resemble those of single-celled organisms like the protozoa?

What I mean by this is that single-celled organisms have simple, binary mechanisms for survival: move toward nutrient, move away from toxin. It turns out that the sea slug, which has one of the most basic nervous systems currently known, utilizes this same two-option approach to lay down memories, a discovery that earned Eric Kandel the Nobel Prize in Physiology in 2000. What about us?

This is not to say that we humans can be reduced to sea slugs. Is it possible, though, that we haven't shrugged off our evolutionary ancestry and indeed take many of our cues from "lower" organisms? Could some (or much) of our behavior be attributed to deeply embedded patterns of approaching that which we find attractive or pleasant, and avoiding that which we find repulsive or unpleasant? And if so, can this knowledge help us change our daily habit patterns, from simple quirks to stubbornly ingrained addictions? Perhaps might we even discover a new way of relating to ourselves and others, one that transcends this basic nature and, ironically, has always been available to our *Homo sapiens sapiens* (she "who knows that she knows") species—that which makes us uniquely human?

Getting Hooked

When we get hooked on the latest video game on our phone, or our favorite flavor of Ben & Jerry's ice cream, we are tapping into one of the most evolutionarily conserved learning processes currently known to science, one shared among countless species and dating back to the most basic nervous systems known to man. This reward-based learning process basically goes like this: We see some food that looks good. Our brain says, *Calories, survival!* And we eat the food. We taste it, it tastes good, and especially when we eat sugar, our bodies send a signal to our brains: remember what you are eating and where you found it. We lay down this memory—based on experience and location (in the lingo: *context*-dependent memory), and we learn to repeat the process the next time. See food. Eat food. Feel good. Repeat. *Trigger, behavior, reward.* Simple, right?

After a while, our creative brains tell us: *Hey! You can use this for more than remembering where food is.* The next time you feel bad, why don't you try eating something good so that you will feel better? We thank our brains for that great idea, try it, and quickly learn that if we eat ice cream or chocolate when we are mad or sad, we do feel better. It is the same learning process, just a different trigger: instead of a hunger signal coming from our stomach, this emotional signal—feeling sad—triggers the urge to eat.

Or maybe in our teenage years we saw the rebel kids smoking outside school and looking cool, and we thought, hey, I want to be like them, and so we started smoking. See cool. Smoke to be cool. Feel good. Repeat. *Trigger, behavior, reward.* And each time we perform the behavior, we reinforce this brain pathway, which says, *Great, do it again.* So we do, and it becomes a habit. A *habit loop.*

Later, feeling stressed out triggers that urge to eat something sweet or to smoke. Now with the same brain mechanisms, we have gone from learning to survive to literally killing ourselves with these habits. Obesity and smoking are among the leading preventable causes of morbidity and mortality in the world.

How did we get into this mess?

From Sea Slugs to Siberian Huskies

The earliest descriptions of this trigger-behavior-reward habit loop were published in the late nineteenth century by a gentleman named Edward Thorndike.[1] He was annoyed by an endless stream of stories about a most curious phenomenon—lost dogs that, against all odds, again and again found their way home. Thorndike, who considered the usual explanations lacking in scientific rigor, set out to research the nuts and bolts of how animals actually learned. In an article entitled "Animal Intelligence," he challenged his colleagues: "Most of these books do not give us a *psychology*, but rather a *eulogy* of animals" (emphasis in the original). He asserted that the scientists of his time had "looked for the intelligent and unusual and neglected the stupid and normal." And by normal, he meant the normal types of learned associations that could be observed in everyday life, in not only dogs but humans as well—for example, hearing the subtle clink of glass on the front porch in the morning and associating that with the milkman having just delivered the day's milk.

In setting out to fill that gap, Thorndike took dogs, cats, and (seemingly less successfully) chicks, deprived them of food, and then put them in various types of cages. These cages were rigged with different types of simple escape mechanisms, such as "pulling at a loop of cord, pressing a lever, or stepping on a platform." Once the animal escaped, it was rewarded with food. He recorded how the animal succeeded in escaping and how long this took. He then repeated the experiment over and over and plotted how many attempts it took for each animal to learn to associate a particular behavior with escape and subsequent food (reward). Thorndike observed, "When the association was thus perfect, the time taken to escape was, of course, practically constant and very short."

Thorndike showed that animals could learn simple behaviors (pull a cord) to get rewards (food). He was mapping out reward-based learning! It is important to note that his methods reduced the influences of observers and other factors that might confound the experiments. He concluded, "Therefore the work done by one investigator may be repeated and verified or modified by another"—which moved the field from writing unexplained stories about the amazing dog that did x, to how we can train all of our dogs (and cats, birds, and elephants) to do x, y, or z.

In the mid-twentieth century, B. F. Skinner reinforced these observations with a series of experiments on pigeons and rats, in which he could carefully measure responses to single changes in conditions (such as the color of the chamber, which became known as a "Skinner box").[2] For example, he could easily train an animal to prefer a black chamber to a white one by feeding it in the former and/or providing

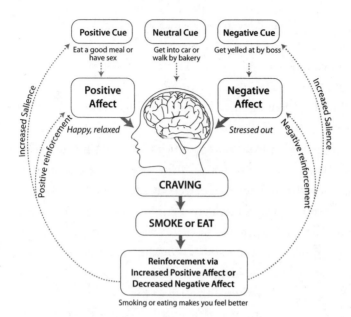

Reward-based learning. Copyright © Judson Brewer, 2014.

small electrical shocks in the latter. He and other scientists extended these findings to show that animals could be trained to perform a behavior not only to gain a reward, but also to avoid a punishment. These approach and avoidance behaviors soon became known as *positive* and *negative* reinforcement, and they became part of the larger concept of "operant conditioning"—the more scientific-sounding name for reward-based learning.

With these insights, Skinner introduced a simple explanatory model that was not only reproducible but also broad and powerful in its ability to explain behavior: we approach stimuli that have been previously associated with something pleasant (reward) and avoid stimuli that have been previously associated with something unpleasant (punishment). He propelled reward-based learning from sideshow to spotlight. These concepts—positive and negative reinforcement (reward-based learning)—are now taught in college introductory psychology courses across the world. This was a breakthrough.

Often heralded as the father of reward-based learning (operant conditioning), Skinner became convinced that much of human behavior beyond simple survival mechanisms could be explained by this process. In fact, in 1948, riffing on Henry David Thoreau's *Walden,* Skinner wrote a novel titled *Walden Two,* in which he describes a utopian society that at every step of the way uses reward-based learning to train people to live in harmony. The novel is a sort of philosophical fiction in which a protagonist named Frazier (an obvious stand-in for Skinner) uses Socratic methods to educate a little troupe of visitors (representing different antagonistic viewpoints) about Walden Two in his attempt to convince them that humans' natural capacity for reward-based learning can be effectively tapped for flourishing over folly.

In the novel, the citizens of this fictional community use "behavioral engineering" (reward-based learning) to shape behavior, beginning at birth. For example, young children learn the rewards of collaboration over competition so that they will become conditioned to habitually prefer the former when a situation arises to choose between the two. In this way, the entire community had been conditioned to behave most efficiently and harmoniously for the good of both the individual and society, because everyone was inextricably linked. One way that *Walden Two* looked at the conditions for social harmony was by scientifically investigating societal norms and *subjective biases*—individual conditioning set up through reward-based learning.

Let's pause and unpack subjective bias a little, because it is a critical piece of this book. Simply put, the more that a behavior is repeated, the more we learn *to see* the world a certain way—through a lens that is *biased,* based on rewards and punishments from previous actions. We form a habit of sorts, the lens being a habitual way of seeing. A simple example: if we eat chocolate and it tastes good, in the future, when given a choice between it and some other sweet that we don't like as much, we will likely lean toward the chocolate. We have learned to wear "chocolate is good" glasses; we have developed a chocolate *bias,* and it is *subjective* because it is particular to our tastes. In the same sense, someone else might have a bias for ice cream over chocolate, and so on. Over time, the more we get used to wearing a particular set of glasses, subscribing to a particular worldview more and more, we forget that we are wearing them. They have become an extension of us—a habit or even a truth. Because subjective bias stems from our core reward-based learning process, it extends well beyond food preferences.

For example, many Americans who grew up in the 1930s learned that a woman's place is in the home. They were likely raised by a stay-at-home mother and perhaps even were negatively reinforced by being scolded or "educated" if they asked why mom was at home and dad was at work ("Honey, your father has to earn money for us to eat."). Over time, our viewpoints become so habitual that we don't question our reflexive, knee-jerk reactions—of course a woman's place is in the home! The term "knee-jerk" comes from medicine: when a physician taps the tendon connecting the knee to the shin with a reflex hammer, she (if you hesitated or tripped on the word "she," it may indicate a subjective bias that doctors should be male) is testing the nerve loop that travels only as far as the level of the spinal cord, never making it to the brain. It requires only *three* cells to complete the circuit (one sensing the tap of the reflex hammer and sending a signal to the spinal cord, one relaying the signal in the spinal cord, and one transmitting the signal to the muscle telling it to contract). Analogously, we spend much of our lives mindlessly and reflexively reacting in accordance with our subjective biases, losing sight of changes in ourselves and our environment that no longer support our habitual actions—which can lead to trouble. If we can understand how subjective bias is set up and operates, we can learn to optimize its utility and minimize any damage it may cause.

For example, the community in *Walden Two* investigated whether women could perform jobs outside their established roles of housewife or elementary school teacher (remember, he wrote this in 1948). When men and women looked beyond their subjective bias of "women perform *x* and *y* roles in society," they saw that indeed women were equally capable of performing the same functions as men—and thus added them to the workforce (while also including men more in child-rearing roles).

Skinner argued that behavioral engineering could help prevent a society from becoming too subjectively biased, which might result in it becoming dysfunctionally hardened in its social structure or dogmatically rigid about its politics. Those kinds of maladjustments happen naturally when the principles of reward-based learning are left unchecked and a few people in key positions use them to manipulate the masses. As we go through this book, we will see whether Skinner's ideas are farfetched or how far they might extend to human behavior.

As *Walden Two* asks philosophically, is there a way that we can remove or at least reduce the amount of subjective bias that conditions our behavior, whether we are sales representatives, scientists, or stockbrokers? Can understanding how our biases are molded and reinforced improve our personal and social lives, and even help us overcome addictions? And what truly human capacities and ways of being emerge once we step out of our old sea slug habit modes?

When I founded the Yale Therapeutic Neuroscience Clinic, my first clinical study was to determine whether mindfulness training could help people quit smoking. I can admit now that I was pretty anxious. Not that I thought mindfulness wouldn't work, but I was worried about my own credibility. You see, I had never smoked.

We recruited study participants to the clinic by handing out matchbooks all over the New Haven, Connecticut, area that read: "Quit smoking without medications." Smokers at the first group session would sit around fidgeting in their chairs, not knowing what they were getting into—this was a randomized blind study, meaning they knew only that they would be getting *some* type of treatment. I would then start talking about how I was going to help them quit smoking by getting them to simply pay attention. That declaration usually elicited a bunch of quizzical looks and set off a new round of fidgeting. At this point, someone would invariably interrupt me and ask, "Dr. Brewer, um, er, have you ever smoked?" They had tried everything else, and now had to listen to some privileged white male nerd from Yale who clearly couldn't relate to their problems.

I would answer, "No, I've never smoked, but I have plenty of addictions." Their eyes would start looking around in desperation for the exit. I tried to reassure them, "And if you can't tell that by the end of the session tonight, please call me out on it." I would then go up to the whiteboard (blocking the exit so that they couldn't escape) and walk them through how the habit of smoking gets set up and reinforced. Because of my experience of working with my own addictive habits and what I had learned from Skinner, I could lay out the common elements of *all* addictions, including smoking.

It took only five minutes of writing on the board, yet by the end they would all be nodding in agreement. The fidgeting was replaced by sighs of relief. They finally understood that I really knew what they were struggling with. Over several years, this question—have I ever smoked?—came up regularly, but the participants never doubted my ability to relate to their experience. Because we all can. It is simply a matter of seeing the patterns.

It turns out that people who smoke are no different from anyone else. Except that they smoke. By this, I mean that we all use the same basic brain processes to form habits: learning to dress ourselves in the morning, checking our Twitter feeds, and smoking cigarettes. This is good and bad news. The bad news is that any of us can get into the habit of excessively checking our e-mail or Facebook accounts throughout the day, slowing down our productivity and decreasing our well-being. The good news is that if we can understand these processes at their core, we can learn to let go of bad habits and foster good ones.

Understanding the underlying psychological and neurobiological mechanisms may help this relearning process be a simpler, though not necessarily easier, task than we think. Some clues about how to do this may come from what my lab has been discovering about how mindfulness—paying attention to our moment-to-moment experience in a particular way—helps us work with our habits. Other clues come from the over twenty thousand people who have taken our eight-week Mindfulness-Based Stress Reduction (MBSR) course at the University of Massachusetts Medical School's Center for Mindfulness.

How Does Paying Attention Help?

Remember the examples of eating chocolate or smoking? We develop all types of learned associations that fail to address that core problem of *wanting to feel better* when we are stressed out or just don't feel great. Instead of examining the root of the problem, we reinforce our subjective biases, prompted by past conditioning: "Oh, maybe I just need *more* chocolate, and then I'll feel better." Eventually, when we have tried everything, including overdosing on chocolate (or worse), we become despondent. Beating the dead horse only makes things worse. Unnerved and feeling lost, we no longer know in which direction to look or turn. Having heard from their doctors, family members, or friends, or even having learned something about the underlying science of stress and addiction, people come to our clinic and take the course.

Many of our MBSR participants are dealing with acute or chronic medical issues, yet broadly speaking, they all share some type of disease. Something is not quite right in their lives, and they are searching for a way to cope, a way to feel better. Often, they have tried many things, without finding anything that fixes the problem. As in the chocolate example above, something works *for a little while,* and then, infuriatingly, its effects die down or stop working altogether. Why are these temporary fixes only temporary?

If we try to reinforce our habits through simple principles of reward-based learning, but our efforts to change them only make matters worse, a good place to start looking for the problem may be to check our assumptions. Stopping and reexamining the subjective biases and habits that we have been carrying around to ease our predicaments helps us see what might be weighing us down (and getting us more lost).

How might mindfulness help us find our way? When learning to backpack in college, I had to navigate in the wilderness for weeks without the help of technology such as my smartphone, and one of the first and most critical skills I learned was how to read a map. Rule number one is that a map is useless if we don't know how to orient it correctly. In other words, we can use a map only if we pair it with a compass to tell us where north is. When our map is oriented, the landmarks fall into place and begin to make sense. Only then can we navigate through the wild.

Similarly, if we have been carrying around a this-isn't-quite-right feeling of dis-ease, and we lack a compass to help us orient to where it is coming from, the disconnection can lead to quite a bit of stress. Sometimes the dis-ease and a lack of awareness of its root cause are so maddening that they lead to a quarter-life or midlife crisis. We fumble around and take extreme measures to shake off the feelings of frustration and dis-ease—the male stereotypical response being to run off with a secretary or an assistant (only to wonder what the hell we have done when we wake up from all the excitement a month later). What if, instead of trying to shake it or beat it, we joined it? In other words, what if we used our feeling of stress or dis-ease *as our compass?* The goal is not to find more stress (we all have plenty of that!), but to use our existing stress as a navigation tool. What does stress *actually feel like,* and how does it differ from other emotions such as excitement? If we can clearly orient ourselves to the needle of "south" (toward stress) and "north" (away from stress), we can use that alignment as a compass to help guide our lives.

What about the map?

There are many definitions of mindfulness. Perhaps the one most often quoted is Jon Kabat-Zinn's operational definition from *Full Catastrophe Living,* which is taught in MBSR classes around the world: "The awareness that arises from paying attention, on purpose, in the present moment, and non-judgmentally."[3] As Stephen Batchelor recently wrote, this definition points toward a "human capability" of "learning how to stabilize attention and dwell in a lucid space of non-reactive awareness."[4] Put differently, mindfulness is about seeing the world more clearly. If we get lost because our subjective biases keep us wandering around in circles, mindfulness brings awareness of *these very biases* so that we can see how we are leading ourselves astray. Once we see that we are not going anywhere, we can stop, drop the unnec-essary baggage, and reorient ourselves. Metaphorically, mindfulness becomes the map that helps us navigate life's terrain.

What do we mean by nonjudgmental or nonreactive awareness? In this book, we will first unpack how reward-based learning leads to subjective bias, and how this bias distorts our view of the world, mov-ing us away from seeing the nature of phenomena clearly and toward habitual reactivity—going along on autopilot by heading toward "nu-trients" and avoiding toxins based on how we reacted previously. We will also explore how this biased view often causes much confusion as well as the reaction "this feels really bad, do something!" which simply compounds the problem. When we are lost in the forest and start panicking, the instinct is to start moving faster. This, of course, often leads to us getting *more* lost.

If I got lost while backpacking, I was taught to stop, take a deep breath, and pull out my map and compass. Only when I was reori-ented and had a clear sense of direction was I supposed to start mov-ing again. This was counter to my instincts, but was (and is) literally lifesaving. Similarly, we will bring the concepts of clear seeing and nonreactivity together to help us learn how we might be compound-ing our own dis-ease, and also learn how to navigate away from it by working with it more skillfully.

Over the last decade, my lab has collected data from "normal" in-dividuals (whatever that means), patients (usually with addictions), people taking the MBSR course at the UMass Center for Mindfulness, and novice and experienced meditators. We have studied addictions of all kinds, different types of meditation and meditators (including Christian "centering prayer" and Zen), and diverse ways of delivering mindfulness training. Over and over our results have fit into and supported this theoretical framework, whether viewed through the ancient Buddhist mindfulness lens or the more modern operant-conditioning lens—or both together.

With these parallels between ancient and modern science as a guide, we will explore how mindfulness helps us see through our learned associations, subjective biases, and the resultant reactivity. As Batchelor puts it, "The point is to gain practical knowledge that leads to changes in behavior that affects the quality of your life; theoretical knowledge in contrast, may have little, if any, impact on how you live in the world from day to day. In letting go of self-centered reactivity, a person gradually comes 'to dwell pervading the entire world with a mind imbued with loving kindness, compassion, altruistic joy, and equanimity.'"[5] This may sound too good to be true, yet we now have good data to back it up.

We will explore how mindfulness helps us read, and therefore make use of, the stress compass so that we can learn to find our way when we have lost it, whether by reactively yelling at our spouse, habitually watching YouTube videos out of boredom, or hitting rock bottom with an addiction. We can move from reacting like a sea slug to being fully human.

PART ONE

The Dopamine Hit

• • •

1

Addiction, Straight Up

When we scratch the wound and give into our addictions we do not allow the wound to heal. But when we instead experience the raw quality of the itch or pain of the wound and do not scratch it, we actually allow the wound to heal. So not giving in to our addictions is about healing at a very basic level.

—*Pema Chödrön*

You can observe a lot by watching.

—*Yogi Berra*

As part of my assistant professorship at the Yale School of Medicine, I worked as an outpatient psychiatrist at the Veterans Administration Hospital (the VA) in West Haven, Connecticut, for five years. I specialized in addiction psychiatry—a field I never imagined joining until I saw very clear connections between mindfulness and improving the lives of my patients. My office was located at the very back of the employee parking lot in a "temporary" building that had somehow, long ago, become permanent. As with all ancillary buildings on the hospital campus, it was known only by a number: Building #36.

Building #36 was the home of our methadone clinic. The first thing patients or visitors saw when they walked into the lobby was a thick piece of bulletproof glass behind which a nurse would stand every morning, doling out methadone in Dixie cups to our patients with opioid addictions. As a rule, when patients arrived for their appointments, the receptionist had to first call the clinician so that we could escort them to our offices. Our clinic had seen everything under the sun, so standard operating procedure was to be safe rather than sorry.

Thanks to Hollywood films like *Leaving Las Vegas* and *Requiem for a Dream,* addicts are frequently shown committing self-destructive acts while drunk or high, or engaging in crime as a means of financing their addictions. Melodrama sells tickets. The vast majority of my patients did not fit these stereotypes. They had their war stories, but theirs were those of everyday life: getting hooked on drugs one way or another and later desperately trying to kick their habits so that they could find stable homes, jobs, and relationships. Addiction is an all-consuming obsession.

Before we continue, a definition of addiction is in order. During my residency training, I learned perhaps the most straightforward of guidelines: addiction is continued use, despite adverse consequences. If something was going wrong related to our use of a particular substance or a specific behavior—whether nicotine, alcohol, cocaine, gambling, or something else—and we nonetheless kept it up, it was grounds for evaluation. The degree to which it turned our lives and those around us upside down helps determine the level of severity. In this way, we can view addictions along a spectrum calibrated as much on the degree to which our behaviors affect our lives as on the behaviors themselves.

Many of my patients at the VA became addicted to drugs after being injured (in battle or elsewhere). Sometimes they were dealing with chronic physical pain and got hooked on opioids as a way to numb it. Other times they had found that drugs were a way to escape, avoid, or dull emotional pain, trauma related or otherwise. When my patients told me their stories of getting addicted, there was a common theme. It was as if they had been one of the lab rats in Skinner's experiments and were describing the reward-based learning process that they had gone through; "I would have a flashback [to some traumatic event]" (trigger), "get drunk" (behavior), "and this was better than reliving the experience" (reward). I could line up their habit loop in my head. *Trigger. Behavior. Reward.* Repeat. In addition, they used substances as a way to "medicate"; by being drunk or high, they could prevent (or avoid) unpleasant memories or feelings from coming up, or not remember afterward whether those memories had surfaced.

My patients and I began our work together by my asking them what initiated their addiction and what was sustaining it. I had to be able to clearly see all aspects of their habit in order to have any hope of treating it. I needed to know what their triggers were, what drugs they were using, and especially, what reward they were getting from using. Something had gone so wrong with their drug use or consequent behavior that they were talking to a psychiatrist—not how most people choose to spend their day. The visit to the VA usually came at the prompting of a primary care provider who was worried about their physical health, or a family member who was worried about their mental health (or perhaps their own safety). If my patient and I couldn't work out what reward they thought that they were getting from their behavior, it would be hard to change it. Addiction rides an evolutionary juggernaut: every abused drug hijacks the dopamine reward system.

For the vast majority of my patients, the reward came from making something unpleasant go away (negative reinforcement). Rarely did one of them say that it felt great to go on a three-day cocaine binge, blow hundreds of dollars or more a day, and sleep it off for the next few days. They described their reward-based learning as a way to avoid situations, numb their pain, mask unpleasant emotions, and, most often, succumb to their cravings. Scratching that damn itch.

Many of my patients, having already conquered one or more of other addictions, came to me to help them quit smoking. With cocaine, heroin, alcohol, or another hard drug, they had hit rock bottom enough times that their family, work, and health problems finally had outweighed the rewards of using. The itch to use couldn't compete with the pile of trouble that came with scratching. At such times, their negative reinforcement for using (trouble) was at last greater than the previous reward (appeasing a craving). They would sit in my office and look at their pack of cigarettes, clearly puzzled. "Why," they would ask me, "if I can quit all these hard drugs on my own, can't I quit smoking?" Their questions were not unique: in one study, almost two-thirds of people seeking treatment for alcohol or other substance-abuse disorders reported that it would be harder to quit cigarettes than their current substance.[1]

As a historical footnote, cigarettes were given to soldiers during World War I to boost morale and help them psychologically escape from their current circumstances. In World War II, four cigarettes were given to soldiers *at each meal* as part of their K rations, a practice that continued until 1975. If I wanted to get someone hooked on cigarettes, that is what I would do. Wartime being a whopper of a stressor (trigger), I would make sure someone could easily smoke cigarettes (behavior) so that they could feel better (reward). Even after a war was over, the addiction already having taken hold, memories, flashbacks, or even simple everyday stressors would keep them coming back for more.

Nicotine has several advantages over other addictive substances in getting and keeping us hooked. These may contribute to the trouble my patients have with quitting.

First, nicotine is a stimulant, so it doesn't dull our cognitive capacity. We can smoke when we drive. We can smoke when operating heavy machinery.

Second, we can smoke throughout the day if we want to. We can smoke when we first get up in the morning (when our nicotine levels are the lowest and we are jonesing for a cigarette). We can smoke on the way to work. We can smoke during breaks, or when we get yelled at by our boss. And so on. Someone who smokes a pack of cigarettes a day can reinforce his or her habit twenty times in a single day.

Third, we can't get fired for smoking on the job. Coming to work high or drunk is a different story. Taking breaks to smoke may cut down a little on our productivity, but we are harming only our personal health, and that is up to us (in theory).

Fourth, although cigarette smoking is currently the leading cause of preventable morbidity and mortality in the United States, cigarettes don't kill us quickly. We lose jobs and relationships much more quickly when we are drunk or high all of the time. Sure, a smoker's breath is pretty bad, but this can be covered with gum or mints. All the other changes that come with smoking come so slowly that we don't notice. It is only after several decades or more of perpetuating the habit that we start to run into major medical problems such as emphysema or cancer. Reward-based learning is about immediate reinforcement, and our long-term-planning mind can't compete with what is right in front of our face when we *might* get cancer *in the future*. We *might* be one of the ones that don't get cancer.

Fifth, capillaries, the smallest blood vessels in our bodies, which deliver the nicotine into the bloodstream, are vast and numerous.

Laid out in rows, the capillaries in our lungs alone would cover the area of a tennis court, or more. With this much surface area, they can rapidly get nicotine into the bloodstream. The more rapidly nicotine gets into the blood, the more rapidly dopamine is released in the brain and the more we get hooked. This ability of the lungs to deliver large amounts of inhaled substances at lightning speed is also why crack cocaine (which is smoked) is more addictive than snorted cocaine. Our noses can't compete with our lungs on the capillary level. Given all these factors, along with others, it is not surprising in the least that my patients, having conquered many demons, can't kick their smoking habits.

Here is a brief case study. Jack walked into my office and told me he felt as though his head would explode if he didn't smoke. He has smoked his whole life and can't stop. He has tried nicotine gum and patches. He has tried eating candy instead of smoking when he gets a craving. Yet nothing has worked. I know from reading the studies that medications *at best* help only about a third of patients stay smoke free. I know from the studies that these meds haven't been shown to help cravings induced by triggers. Medications mostly help either by providing a steady supply of nicotine, leading to a *steady supply* of dopamine, or else by blocking the receptor that nicotine attaches to so that dopamine doesn't get released when someone smokes. These mechanisms make sense: an ideal drug would be one that *quickly releases* a surge of dopamine, yet only when we recognize our specific triggers. We are not quite yet at that level of personalized medicine.

Standing in the doorway of my office, Jack genuinely looked to be at his wit's end—as if his head *were* going to explode. What was I supposed to say or do? I started by cracking a joke. Perhaps not the best idea, given my track record with jokes, but it just fell out of my mouth. "When your head does explode," I stammered, "pick up the pieces, put them back together, and give me a call. We'll document it as the first case of a head explosion caused by a craving." He politely laughed (at least my VA patients were kind—despite or perhaps because of all they had been through, they had huge hearts). Now what? I went to the whiteboard on my office wall and walked Jack through the habit loop. Standing next to each other, together we diagrammed his triggers that led to smoking, and how each time he smoked he reinforced the process. He was nodding at this point and sat down. Progress.

I went back and explored Jack's feeling that his head would explode if he didn't smoke. I asked him what that was like. At first he said, "I don't know, like my head will explode." I then asked him to carefully detail what this actually felt like. We started to distill all his thoughts and physical sensations when he felt a strong craving come on. I then drew a wide arrow on the whiteboard and plotted his body sensations on it.

Starting with the trigger at the bottom, we added points along the line as his craving sensations grew stronger and more pronounced. The tip of the arrow was supposed to point to his head exploding, but that point was instead replaced by smoking a cigarette. Because every time he got to that point, he snapped and smoked.

Then I asked whether there ever had been times when he couldn't smoke—on an airplane or a bus, for example. Yes, he replied. "What happened then?" I asked. He pondered for a few moments and said something to the effect of, "I guess it went away." "Let me make sure I understand," I said. "If you don't smoke, your cravings go away on their own?" I was leading the witness, but to be fair, I did want to make sure I understood him. We had to be on the same page in order to proceed. He nodded.

I went back to the arrow that I had drawn on the whiteboard, and just below the tip (which signified his smoking a cigarette), I extended the line horizontally and then back down. The whole thing looked like an inverted *U* or a hump instead of an arrow pointing in a single direction toward a cigarette.

"Is this what you mean? You get triggered, and your craving builds, crests, and then falls as it goes away?" I asked. I could see the lightbulb go on in Jack's head. Wait a minute. When necessary, he had made it without smoking, but hadn't realized it. Some of his cravings were short, and others lasted longer, but *all* of them went away. Perhaps quitting *was* something he could do after all.

Over the next few minutes, I made sure he really understood how each time that he smoked, he reinforced his habit. I taught him to simply note to himself (silently or aloud) each body sensation that came on with a craving. We used the analogy of surfing: my patient's cravings were like waves, and he could use this "noting practice" as a surfboard to help him get on the wave and ride it until it was gone. He could ride the wave as if it were the inverted *U* on the board, feeling it build, crest, and fall. I explained how each time he rode the wave, he stopped reinforcing the habit of smoking. He now had a concrete tool—his own surfboard—that he could use each time he craved a smoke.

Surf's Up!

The practice that I gave to Jack to help him quit smoking didn't come out of thin air. When I started working at the VA, I had been steadily meditating for about twelve years. And during my residency training at the Yale School of Medicine, I had made the decision to discontinue molecular biology research and shift the research part of my career to studying mindfulness full-time. Why? Although I had published my graduate work linking stress to immune system dysregulation in high-profile journals, and had even had some of the work patented, I was still left with the "so what" question. All my work had been in mouse models of disease. How did those findings directly help humans? At the same time, I was really seeing the benefit of mindfulness in my personal life. That awareness had directly informed my decision to train to become a psychiatrist. More and more, I saw clear connections between Buddhist teachings and the psychiatric frameworks that we were using to better understand and treat our patients. My switch to studying mindfulness didn't go over so well with the faculty, which was generally dubious of anything that didn't come in pill form or had even a whiff of alternative medicine about it. And I don't blame them. Psychiatry has been fighting many uphill battles for a long time, including the one of legitimacy.

In 2006, a few years before starting my stint at the VA and during my psychiatry residency training, I performed my first pilot study to see whether mindfulness training could help people with addictions.[2] Alan Marlatt's group at the University of Washington had recently published a study showing that Mindfulness-Based Relapse Prevention (MBRP), a combination of MBSR and a relapse prevention program that he had developed, could help prevent people from slipping back into their addictions. With their help, I modified the eight-week MBRP so that it could be used in our outpatient clinic: I split it into two four-week blocks (A and B) that could be taught in sequence (A-B-A-B- . . .) so that patients wouldn't have to wait long to start treatment. Also, patients who were in their second block of treatment could model and teach folks who were just starting out. Though it was a small study (my statistician jokingly called it the "brown bag study" because I brought her all the data in a brown grocery bag), our results were encouraging. We found that the modified version of MBRP worked as well as cognitive behavioral therapy (CBT) at helping people not relapse into alcohol or cocaine use. Broadly speaking, CBT is an evidence-based therapy that trains people to challenge old assumptions and change thinking patterns (cognitions) in order to improve how they feel and behave. For example, patients who suffer from depression or addiction are taught to "catch it, check it, change it" when they notice negative beliefs about themselves that can lead to drug use. If they have the thought, "I'm terrible," they learn to check to see whether it is true, and then change it to something more positive.

We also found that when we tested patients' reactions to stress (in this case, hearing their recorded stories played back to them) after treatment, those who received mindfulness training didn't react as strongly as those receiving CBT. Mindfulness seemed to help them cope with their cues both in the lab and in real life.

After these encouraging results, I decided to tackle smoking. As mentioned, nicotine addiction is one of the hardest to conquer. Mindfulness approaches had recently been shown to be helpful for chronic pain, depression, and anxiety.[3] If mindfulness could help here as well, it might help usher in new behavioral treatments for addiction (which had been lagging) and help my patients at the same time.

In graduate school, one of my mentors used to give me a big smile and say, "Go big or go home!" He meant that if I was waffling between taking a risk with something outside my comfort level and being conservative and staying within it, I should do the former. Life was too short. With his voice in my head, I stripped out all of Marlatt's relapse prevention components in MBRP and wrote a new manual for our smoking study that consisted solely of mindfulness training. I wanted to see whether mindfulness *by itself* could work. And if it worked for one of the hardest addictions to break, I could feel more comfortable in using mindfulness training with any of my addicted patients.

As part of my preparation for running our smoking study, I started meditating for two-hour stretches, with the aim of not moving until the bell went off. That sounds a bit masochistic, yet this was my reasoning: Nicotine has a half-life of about two hours. Unsurprisingly, most smokers go out for a smoke break about every two hours. Their nicotine levels get low and their brains urge them to fill up the tank. As people cut down, they smoke less frequently, leading to stronger urges, and so forth. We were going to help our smokers slowly wean themselves off cigarettes so that they would be less likely to have physiologically based cravings. (Such training doesn't help with cravings triggered by cues.) And when patients quit altogether, they have to ride out each and every craving, no matter what, if they are going to "stay quit." I was a nonsmoker who needed to be able to relate to patients who felt as though their heads were going to explode unless they smoked. I couldn't be pulling any I'm-the-doctor-so-do-as-I-say nonsense. They had to trust me. They had to believe that I knew what I was talking about.

So I started sitting, without moving, for two hours at a time. Correction: I started *trying* to sit in meditation posture for that length of time. Surprisingly, it wasn't the physical pain of not shifting for a long time that got me. It was the restlessness. My brain urged me to "just shift a little, no biggie." Those cravings shouted, "Get up!" Now I knew (or at least had a much better sense of) what my patients were going through. I knew what it was like to feel as if my head would explode.

I don't remember how many *months* it took before I made it the full two hours. I would get to an hour and forty-five minutes and would get up. I would get almost to the full two hours, and then, like a puppet at the hands of a master named Restlessness, I would pop off the cushion. I simply couldn't do it. Then one day I did. I sat for the full two hours. At that point I knew I could do it. I knew that I could cut the restlessness strings. Each subsequent sit got easier and easier because I had confidence that it could be done. And I knew that my patients could quit smoking. They simply needed the proper tools.

From Craving to Quit

Finally, in 2008, I was ready. As mentioned in the introduction, I launched the Yale Therapeutic Neuroscience Clinic with a smoking cessation study that hoped to answer a simple but elegant question: was mindfulness training as effective as the "gold standard" treatment, the best available—in this case, the American Lung Association's program aptly named "Freedom From Smoking"? We recruited smokers by blanketing the surrounding area with matchbooks advertising a free program that didn't use medication.

People who signed up for the study came to our waiting room on the first night of treatment and drew a piece of paper out of a cowboy hat (my research assistant had a flair for this type of thing). If they drew a "1," they would get mindfulness training. If they drew a "2," they would go through the American Lung Association's "Freedom From Smoking" program. Twice a week for four weeks they would come to treatment. At the end of the month, they would blow into a contraption that looks like a Breathalyzer, to see whether they had quit smoking. Instead of measuring alcohol, our monitor measured carbon monoxide (CO). CO, a by-product of incomplete combustion, is a reasonable surrogate marker for smoking, because a lot of it gets into the bloodstream when we smoke a cigarette. CO binds to the hemoglobin in red blood cells more tightly than oxygen does, which is why we suffocate (asphyxiate) when we sit in a closed garage with the car running. Smoking is a way of doing this more slowly. Because it sticks around in our blood, slowing unbinding from our red blood cells before we can exhale it, CO is a decent marker of smoking.

Every month for the next two years (except during December, a notoriously terrible time for people to try to quit smoking), I taught a new group of recruits mindfulness. In the first class, I would teach them the habit loop. We would map out their triggers and how they reinforced their behavior with each cigarette. I would send them home that evening with an admonition to simply pay attention to their triggers and to what it felt like when they did smoke. They were collecting data.

Three days later, at the second class, people would come back with reports of noticing how many times they smoked out of boredom. One gentleman cut down from thirty cigarettes to ten in those two days because he realized that the majority of his smoking was either habitual or a "solution" to fix other problems. For example, he smoked to cover up the bitter taste of coffee. With this simple realization, he started brushing his teeth instead. Perhaps more interesting were the reports I got from participants about what it was like to pay attention when they smoked. Many of them couldn't believe how their eyes had been opened; they had never realized how bad smoking tasted. One of my favorite responses: "Smells like stinky cheese and tastes like chemicals. *Yuck.*"

This patient knew cognitively that smoking was bad for her. That was why she had joined our program. What she discovered by simply being curious and attentive *when* she smoked was that smoking tastes horrible. This was an important distinction. She moved from knowledge to wisdom, from knowing in her head that smoking was bad to *knowing* it in her bones. The spell of smoking was broken; she started to grow viscerally disenchanted with her behavior. No force necessary.

Why am I mentioning force here? With CBT and related treatments, cognition is used to control behavior—hence the name cognitive behavioral therapy. Unfortunately, the part of our brain best able to consciously regulate behavior, the prefrontal cortex, is the first to go offline when we get stressed. When the prefrontal cortex goes offline, we fall back into old habits. Which is why the kind of disenchantment experienced by my patient is so important. Seeing what we really get from our habits helps us understand them on a deeper level, know it in our bones, without needing to control or force ourselves to hold back from smoking.

This awareness is what mindfulness is all about: seeing clearly what happens when we get caught up in our behaviors and then becoming viscerally disenchanted. Over time, as we learn to see more and more clearly the results of our actions, we let go of old habits and form new ones. The paradox here is that mindfulness is just about being interested in, and getting close and personal with, what is happening in our bodies and minds. It is really this willingness to turn toward our experience rather than to try to make our unpleasant cravings go away as quickly as possible.

After our smokers started to get the hang of being okay with having cravings, and even turning toward them, I taught them how to surf. I used an acronym that a senior meditation teacher named Michelle McDonald had developed (and had been widely taught by Tara Brach), and that I had found helpful during my own mindfulness training. In particular, it helped when I got caught up in some obsessive thought pattern or was stuck yelling at somebody in my head: RAIN.

☐ RECOGNIZE/RELAX into what is arising (for example, your craving)

☐ ACCEPT/ALLOW it to be there

☐ INVESTIGATE bodily sensations, emotions, and thoughts (for example, ask, "What is happening in my body or mind right now?")

☐ NOTE what is happening from moment to moment

The *N* is a slight modification of what I learned as "nonidentification." The idea is that we identify with or get caught up in the object that we are aware of. We take it personally. Nonidentification is a bell in our head that reminds us not to take it personally. Instead of trying to explain all this in class two, I turned to "noting practice," a technique popularized by the late Mahasi Sayadaw, a well-respected Burmese teacher. Many variations are currently taught, but in general during noting practice, someone simply notes whatever is most predominant in his or her experience, whether thoughts, emotions, bodily sensations, or sights and sounds. Noting practice is a pragmatic way to work on nonidentification because when we become aware of an object, we can no longer be identified with it (as much). This phenomenon is similar to the observer effect in physics, in which the act of observation, particularly at the subatomic level, changes what is being observed. In other words, when we notice (and note) the physical sensations arising in our bodies that make up a craving, we become less caught up in the habit loop, simply through that observation.

At the end of the second session, I sent them home with a handout and a wallet-size summary card so that they could start practicing RAIN, the main informal training of the course, which they could use anytime a craving came on.

Box 1

We can learn to ride the waves of wanting by surfing them. First, by **RECOGNIZING** that the wanting or craving is coming, and then **RELAXING** into it. Since you have no control over it coming, **ACKNOWLEDGE** or **ACCEPT** this wave as it is; don't ignore it, distract yourself, or try to do something about it. This is your experience. Find a way that works for you, such as a word or phrase, or a simple nod of the head (I consent, here we go, this is it, etc.). To catch the wave of wanting, you have to study it carefully, **INVESTIGATING** it as it builds. Do this by asking, "**What does my body feel like right now?**" Don't go looking. See what arises most prominently. Let it come to you. Finally, **NOTE** the experience as you follow it. Keep it simple by using short phrases or single words. For example: thinking, restlessness in stomach, rising sensation, burning, etc. Follow it until it completely subsides. If you get distracted, return to the investigation by repeating the question, what does my body feel like right now? See if you can ride it until it is completely gone. Ride it to shore.

After the RAIN

Over the rest of the training sessions, I added in formal meditation practices that were to be done regularly each morning or evening as a foundation for developing and supporting mindfulness throughout the day. We kept logs of what people did and didn't practice each week, and tracked how many cigarettes they smoked each day. Ambitiously, I had set a quit date for the end of week two (session four), which turned out to be a bit early for most folks. Some quit at two weeks and then used the last two weeks to reinforce their tools, and some took a bit longer.

While my patients were learning to quit smoking by using mindfulness, a psychologist trained by the American Lung Association delivered the Freedom From Smoking treatment in another room down the hall. To ensure that we didn't bias any aspect of the training, we swapped rooms every other month. By the end of the two-year period, we had screened over 750 people and randomized just fewer than 100 of them for our trial. When the last subjects completed their final four-month follow-up visits, we took all the data and looked to see how well mindfulness training stacked up.

I was hoping that our novel treatment would work as well as the gold standard. When the data came back from our statisticians, the participants in the mindfulness training group had quit *at twice the rate* of the Freedom From Smoking group. Better yet, nearly all mindfulness participants had stayed quit, while many of those in the other group had lost ground, yielding a fivefold difference between the two! This was much better than I had expected.

Why had mindfulness worked? We taught people to pay attention to their habit loops so that they would become disenchanted with their previous behaviors (smoking) by seeing clearly what rewards they were actually getting (for example, the taste of chemicals). Yet we also taught them other mindfulness exercises such as breath awareness and loving-kindness. Maybe the program participants were distracting themselves with these other practices, or maybe something else entirely was happening that we hadn't anticipated.

I gave a Yale medical student the task of figuring out what accounted for the differences. Sarah Mallik was doing her medical school thesis in my lab; she looked to see whether formal meditation and informal mindfulness practice (such as RAIN) predicted outcomes in either group. She found strong correlations between mindfulness practices and quitting smoking, but no correlations in the Freedom From Smoking group, whose participants listened to a CD that taught them relaxation and other methods of distracting themselves from their cravings. We hypothesized that maybe sitting through difficult meditation periods (as I had done) might help smokers wait out cravings. Or maybe the ability to meditate was simply a marker for individuals who were more likely to use mindfulness. We found that the RAIN practice in the mindfulness group was highly correlated with outcomes, too, whereas the parallel informal practices in the Freedom From Smoking group were not. Maybe RAIN was driving the results. Not knowing the exact answer, we published our results, suggesting all these as possible explanations.[4]

Another medical student, Hani Elwafi, was interested in trying to figure out what made the difference in helping people who used mindfulness quit smoking. If we could pinpoint the psychological mechanism of mindfulness's effect, we would be able to streamline future treatments to focus them on the active components. As an analogy: if we were feeding people chicken soup to help cure a cold, it would be helpful to know whether it was the chicken, the broth, or the carrots that were doing the trick. Then we could make sure they were getting *that* ingredient.

Hani took Sarah's data and started looking to see which of the mindfulness training tools (meditation, RAIN, etc.) had the strongest effect on the relationship between craving and smoking. We looked specifically at the relationship between craving and smoking because craving had been clearly linked as part of the habit loop. Without a craving, people were much less likely to smoke. Hani found that, indeed, before mindfulness training, craving predicted smoking. If people craved a cigarette, they were very likely to smoke one. Yet by the end of the four weeks of training, this relationship had been severed. Interestingly, people who quit reported craving cigarettes at the same level as those that didn't quit. They just didn't smoke when they craved. Over time, their cravings decreased as they quit smoking. This made sense, and in our report we explained it thus:

> A simplistic analogy is that craving is like a fire that is fed by smoking. When someone stops smoking, the fire of craving is still present and only burns down on its own once its fuel has been consumed (and no more fuel has been added). Our data provide direct support for this: (1) a drop in craving lags behind smoking cessation for individuals who quit, suggesting that at first there is residual "fuel" for craving to continue to arise, which then is consumed over time, leading to the observed delay in reduction in craving; and (2) craving continues for individuals who continue to smoke, suggesting that they continually fuel it.[5]

We had lifted this explanation directly from an early Buddhist text, which was rife with fire analogies for craving.[6] Those early meditators were smart.

And finally to our original question: which mindfulness skill was the biggest predictor of breaking the link between craving and smoking? The winner: RAIN. While formal meditation practices were positively correlated with outcomes, the informal practice of RAIN was the only one that passed statistical muster—showing a direct relationship to breaking the craving-smoking link. This story was coming together nicely.

Of Monks and Mechanisms

The more I looked at *why* mindfulness training helped people quit and stay quit, the more I started to understand why other treatments and approaches failed. A number of studies had clearly linked craving and smoking. Avoiding cues (triggers) might help prevent people from being triggered, but didn't directly target the core habit loop. For example, staying away from friends who smoke can be helpful. Yet if getting yelled at by the boss triggered someone to smoke, avoiding the boss might lead to other stressors, such as unemployment. Classical substitution strategies such as eating candy have helped people quit smoking. Though in addition to weight gain (which is common with smoking cessation), this technique trains participants to eat when they have a craving to smoke, effectively trading one vice for another. Our data showed that mindfulness decoupled this link between craving and smoking. Further, decoupling craving and behavior seemed to be important for preventing cues from becoming stronger or more salient triggers. Each time we lay down a memory linking a cue with a behavior, our brain starts looking for the cue *and its friends*—anything similar to that original cue can trigger a craving.

I was curious. In my own exploration of meditation, I had run across a fair number of ancient Buddhist teachings that emphasized working with craving.[7] Target craving and you can conquer an addiction. And this targeting of craving was not through brute force but, counterintuitively, through turning toward or getting close to it. Through direct observation, we can become, as the term *asava* is translated, less "intoxicated." I saw this effect with my patients. They became less enchanted with their intoxicants by directly observing what reward they were getting from acting on their urges. How does this process work, exactly?

Jake Davis is a former Theravada Buddhist monk and a scholar of Pali (the language in which Buddhist teachings were first written down). I first met him after I had finished my residency and joined the Yale faculty. We had met through a friend and colleague, Willoughby Britton, also a meditation practitioner and a researcher at Brown University. At the time, Jake was studying philosophy in graduate school. We quickly hit it off, since neither of us had any interest in talking about non-meditation-related niceties. At some point, I showed him the current psychological models of reward-based learning. These seemed to me much like the Buddhist model of "dependent origination," a concept I had learned about while reading Buddhist texts in graduate school. According to the Pali Canon, the Buddha was said to have been contemplating this idea on the night that he became enlightened. Maybe it was worth looking into further.

Dependent origination describes twelve links of a cause-and-effect loop. Something that happens depends upon something else causing it to happen—literally, "This is, because that is. This is not, because that is not." It had caught my eye because it seemed to be describing operant conditioning, or reward-based learning, 2,500 years ago. It goes like this. When we encounter a sensory experience, our mind interprets it based on our prior experience (which is classically described as "ignorance"). This interpretation automatically generates a "feeling tone" that is experienced as pleasant or unpleasant. The feeling tone leads to a craving or an urge—for the pleasant to continue or the unpleasant to go away. Thus motivated, we act on the urge, which fuels the birth of what is referred to in Buddhist psychology as a self-identity. Interestingly, the term for fuel (*upadana*) is classically translated as "attachment"—which is where Western culture often focuses. The outcome of the action is recorded as a memory,

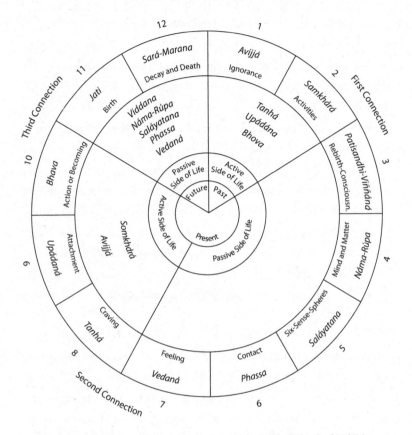

Complex diagram of dependent origination. "The Wheel of Life" by Kalakannija. Licensed under CC BY-SA 4.0 via Wikimedia Commons.

which then conditions the next "round of rebirth," aka samsara, or endless wandering.

This model might sound a little confusing, because it is. Over a period of time, Jake and I unpacked each of these components and found that dependent origination really did line up with reward-based learning. In fact, the two lined up quite beautifully. You see, the steps of dependent origination were essentially the same as those of reward-based learning. They just happened to be called by different names.

Starting at the top, the classical concept of ignorance is very much like the modern idea of subjective bias. We see things a certain way based on memories of our previous experiences. These biases ingrain certain habitual reactions that are typically affective in nature—that is, they involve how something feels emotionally. These unthinking responses correspond to the bit about pleasant and unpleasant as described by dependent origination. If chocolate tasted good to us in the past, seeing it might lead to a pleasant feeling. If we got food poisoning the last time we ate chocolate, we might not feel so good the next time we see it. A pleasant feeling leads to a craving in both models. And in both models, craving leads to behavior or action. So far, so good. Now this is where I needed some help. In dependent origination, behavior leads to "birth." Ancient Buddhists didn't talk explicitly about memory formation (the seat of the mind in ancient times was thought to be in the liver in some cultures, in the heart in others). Could birth be what we now call memory? If we think of how we know who we are, knowledge of our identity is primarily based on memory. Good enough. Of course, the round of rebirth, or endless wandering, fit perfectly. Each time we drink, smoke, or do some other behavior as a way to escape an unpleasant experience, we train ourselves to do it again—without having fixed the problem. If we keep going in that direction, our suffering will continue endlessly.

Jake and I drew up a simplified diagram that stayed true to the form of dependent origination—this is, because that is—yet brought the language into the modern day. We used a pair of glasses to signify the first step in the wheel (ignorance) in order to help people visualize how this biased view of the world filters incoming information and

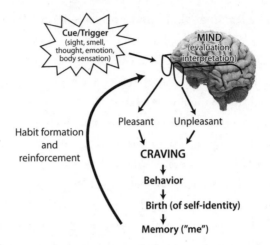

Simplified version of dependent origination.
Copyright © Judson Brewer, 2014.

keeps the wheel spinning, perpetuating the cycle of habit formation and reinforcement.

In addition, we published a paper that used addictions as an example to show scholars, clinicians, and scientists the remarkable similarities between dependent origination and reward-based learning.[8]

After being tested in numerous conference presentations and discussions over the past few years, the models seem to be holding up. They help connect ancient and modern ideas behind potential mechanisms of how our treatments work. It streamlines scholarship when different sets of terms can be linked, since fewer things will then get lost in translation. And from a pure Darwinian, survival-of-the-fittest standpoint, it is oddly reassuring that some psychological models such as dependent origination have stood the test of time, whether they are seen as consistent with new models, rediscovered in the present day, or treated as old wine in new bottles.

In the world of science, reward-based learning goes something like this: develop a theory or discover something new (trigger), be the first to publish an article about it (behavior), and other people will cite your work, you will get promoted, and so forth (reward). There is even an associated term for what happens when someone publishes before us: "getting scooped." Lo and behold, it looks as if the Buddha scooped Skinner, long before paper was invented.

The so-what question that had been kicking around in my mind for years was finally being answered. I could see from my own addictive thinking processes how I set up habits that simply left me thirsty for more. From these insights, I could understand and relate to my patients' problems, and learn how to better treat their addictions. This knowledge led to our clinical trials, which suggested these techniques worked with a wide range of people. That understanding helped us circle back to the beginning—by learning that the modern mechanistic models were the same as those developed thousands of years ago. Could these models help more broadly with behaviors other than hard-core addictions? Could they, in fact, help people in general live better lives?

2

Addicted to Technology

The difference between technology and slavery is that slaves are fully aware that they are not free.

—*Nassim Nicholas Taleb*

In December 2014, my wife and I flew to Paris, where I was scheduled to give a talk about the science of mindfulness. It was our first visit to the City of Lights, so we did what many tourists do: we went to the Louvre. It was a chilly overcast day, yet we were excited to visit the famous museum, which I had read and heard so much about. My wife, a biblical and ancient Near Eastern studies scholar, was especially excited to show me all the ancient wonders collected there. We walked quickly through the narrow streets of the first arrondissement. When we made it through the arches into the courtyard containing the iconic entrance to the museum, lots of people were milling about, eating, and taking pictures. One small group stopped me dead in my tracks. I quickly took a picture of them to capture the scene.

I am not a photographer, so don't judge my aesthetics. What is special about two women taking a selfie? What I found tragic and telling was the slightly slumped gentleman with the hooded jacket in the foreground. He was the boyfriend of one of the women, standing there cold and listless because he had been replaced—by a two-foot-

Taking a selfie at the Louvre. Photograph by the author.

long collapsible aluminum pole. The dis-eased look that I saw on his face expressed his perceived obsolescence.

In 2012, the term "selfie" was one of *Time* magazine's top ten buzzwords. In 2014, the magazine named the "selfie stick" one of its top twenty-five inventions of the year. To me, it's a sign of the apocalypse. Photographic self-portraits date back to the mid-1800s. Why are we so obsessed with taking pictures of ourselves?

Finding the Self in Selfie

Taking the example of the two women in the picture, we can imagine a narrative going on in one of their heads:

WOMAN (THINKING TO HERSELF): "*Mon Dieu!* I'm at the Louvre!"
WOMAN'S MIND CHATTERING BACK TO HER: "Well, don't just
    stand there! Take a picture. No, wait! Take a picture with your

best friend. Stop! I've got it! Take a picture and post it on Facebook!"

WOMAN: "Great idea!"

"Danielle" (let's call her that) snaps the picture, puts her phone away, and then enters the museum to start looking around at the exhibits. Barely ten minutes pass before she gets the urge to check her phone. While her friends are looking away, she steals a furtive glance to see whether anyone has "liked" her picture. Maybe she feels a little guilty, so she quickly puts the phone away before they see her. A few minutes later, the urge hits again. And again. She ends up spending the rest of the afternoon wandering around the Louvre, looking at what? Not the world-famous art, but her Facebook feed, keeping track of how many "likes" and comments she has received. This scenario might sound crazy, but it happens every day. And we may now know why.

Trigger. Behavior. Reward. Since they form the foundation of this book, I frequently reiterate these three ingredients critical to developing a learned behavior. Together, they shape behavior across the animal kingdom, from creatures with the most primitive nervous systems to human beings suffering from addictions (whether crack cocaine or Facebook), and even to societal movements.[1] We can think of reward-based learning as occurring on a spectrum from benign to the most severe. Learning simple habits such as tying our shoes when we are children brings the reward of praise from our parents, or relief from the frustration of not being able to do it ourselves. Toward the other end of the spectrum, becoming obsessed with our phones to the point of texting while driving (which has become as dangerous as being drunk behind the wheel) comes from repeated reinforcement. Somewhere in the middle lies everything from daydreaming to rumination to getting stressed out. We each have stress buttons that get pushed, and what they are largely depends on how we have learned, in a reward-dependent manner, to cope (or not cope) with life. It seems that the degree to which these stressors affect our lives and those around us determines where on the learning spectrum they fall. At the far end of the spectrum lie our addictions—continued use despite adverse consequences. Tying our shoes is a good habit to form. Texting while driving isn't. It is important to note that a clearly defined reward makes all the difference in which behaviors we cultivate, how quickly we learn them, and how strongly they take hold.

According to Skinner, behaviors are shaped in the following way: "Events which are found to be reinforcing are of two sorts. Some reinforcements consist of presenting stimuli, of adding something—for example, food, water, or sexual contact—to the situation. These we call *positive* reinforcers. Others consist of removing something—for example, a loud noise, a very bright light, extreme cold or heat, or electric shock—from the situation. These we call *negative* reinforcers. In both cases the effect of reinforcement is the same—the probability of response is increased."[2] Simply put, we, like other organisms, learn to engage in activities that result in positive outcomes, and avoid those that result in negative ones. The more unambiguously the action is linked to the reward, the more it is reinforced.

Danielle, our Louvre-going lady, doesn't realize that she has fallen for the oldest trick in the evolutionary book. Each time that she has an urge to post another picture to Facebook (trigger), posts it (behavior), and gets a bunch of likes (reward), she perpetuates the process. Consciously or unconsciously, she reinforces her behavior. Instead of soaking up the rich history of the Louvre, Danielle stumbles around like an addict in a daze, looking for her next hit. How common is this obsessive activity, and is it contributing to a more "me-centered" culture?

YouTube = MeTube

"Status Update," an episode of the podcast *This American Life,* featured three ninth graders talking about their use of Instagram. Instagram is a simple program that lets people post, comment on, and share pictures. Simple but valuable: in 2012, Instagram was bought by Facebook for one *billion* dollars.

The podcast episode began with the teens hanging out, waiting for the interview to start. What did they do? They took pictures of themselves and posted them on Instagram. The story went on to describe how they spend much of their day posting pictures, commenting on them, or "liking" those of their friends. One of the girls noted, "Everyone's always on Instagram," and another chimed in, "There's definitely a weird psychology to it . . . It's just sort of the way it is. It's like unspoken rules that everybody knows and follows."

Later in the interview, they described their behavior as "mindless." The host, Ira Glass, then asked an interesting question: "And so, since it's mindless, does it still work? Does it make you feel good?" Despite one girl admitting, "I 'like' everything on my feed" (that is, she clicks the "like" button regardless of what the picture is), the teens all agreed that getting those likes still made them feel good. One concluded, "That's, like, human nature."

Even though they described their activity as rote and mindless, something about it was rewarding. Rats press levers for food. This trio presses buttons for likes. Perhaps this reward isn't just about taking pictures, but is instead dependent on the *subject* of the picture—ourselves. Does this subject provide enough of a reward to keep us coming back for more?

Neuroscience may have insight into the human nature that these teens spoke of. Diana Tamir and Jason Mitchell at Harvard performed a simple study: they put people in a functional magnetic resonance imaging (fMRI) scanner and gave them the choice of reporting their own opinions and attitudes, judging the attitudes of another person, or answering a trivia question.[3] Participants in the study repeated this task almost two hundred times. All the while, their brain activity was being measured. The catch was that the choices were associated with monetary payoffs. For example, in one trial, they might be given a choice between answering a question about themselves or about somebody else, and earn x dollars for choosing the former versus y dollars for the latter. The amount of money was varied, as was the category with which the bigger payoff was associated. At the end of the study, once all the payoffs had been tallied, the scientists could determine whether people were willing to give up money to talk about themselves.

And they were. On average, participants lost an average of 17 percent of potential earnings to think and talk about themselves! Just think about this for a second. Why would anyone give up good money to do this? Not unlike people who forgo job and family responsibilities because of substance abuse, these participants activated their nucleus accumbens while performing the task. Is it possible that the same brain region that lights up when someone smokes crack cocaine or uses any other drug of abuse is also activated when people talk about themselves? In fact, the nucleus accumbens is one of the brain regions most consistently linked to the development of addictions. So there seems to be a link between the self and reward. Talking about ourselves is rewarding, and doing it obsessively may be very similar to getting hooked on drugs.

A second study took this one step further.[4] Dar Meshi and colleagues at the Freie Universität Berlin measured volunteers' brain activity while they received varying amounts of positive feedback about themselves (or about a stranger, as a control condition). As in the Harvard study, they found that participants' nucleus accumbens became more active when receiving self-relevant feedback. The researchers also had the participants fill out a questionnaire that determined a "Facebook intensity" score, which included the number of their Facebook friends and the amount of time they spent on Facebook each day (the maximum score was more than three hours a day). When they correlated nucleus accumbens activity with Facebook intensity, they found that the amount that this brain region lit up *predicted* the intensity of Facebook use. In other words, the more active the nucleus accumbens, the more likely someone was to spend time on Facebook.

A third study, by Lauren Sherman and colleagues at UCLA, topped this off by measuring adolescents' brain activity while they were viewing a simulated Instagram "feed" consisting of a string of pictures they submitted, as well as those of their "peers" (which were provided by the research team). To mimic Instagram as accurately as possible, the picture feed displayed the number of likes that participants' pictures had garnered. The twist was that the researchers had randomly split the pictures into two groups and assigned a certain number of likes to each one: many versus few. Because much of peer endorsement is online, and thus unambiguously *quantifiable* (for example, like versus no like), the researchers used this experimental manipulation so that they could measure the effect of this type of peer interaction on brain activity. This setup is different from face-to-face interaction, which involves bringing together context, nonverbal facial and body cues, and tone of voice (among other factors), which together leave a lot of room for ambiguity and subjective interpretation. Questions such as "why did she look at me that way?" and "what did she *really* mean when she said that?" are a constant source of teen angst. In other words, how does the clear, quantitative peer feedback that adolescents receive through social media affect the brain? In line with the first two studies, adolescent brains showed significantly greater activation in the nucleus accumbens as well as in a brain region implicated in self-reference (more on this in later chapters).[5]

The take-home message from these studies is that there seems to be something biologically rewarding about talking and getting (clear) feedback about ourselves—likely the same type of reward that drives the addictive process. YouTube is named *You*Tube after all.

Why would our brains be set up so that we get a reward when we receive feedback—or even just think about ourselves? Our teenage friends from the *This American Life* episode may give us a clue:

JULIA (TEENAGER): "It's like I'm—I'm a brand."

ELLA (TEENAGER): "You're trying to promote yourself."

JULIA: "The brand. I'm the director of the—"

IRA GLASS (HOST): "And you're the product."

JANE (TEENAGER): "You're definitely trying to promote yourself."

JULIA: "To stay relevant . . ."

They then dove into a conversation about relevance. They joked about how they were "really relevant" in middle school because their social circles were set. Their social groups and friends were known, stable. The ground rules of social engagement were established. There was little ambiguity—at least, as little as there can be in a teenager's mind. But at three months into high school, their circle of friends and their social groups were uncertain, up for grabs. As Glass put it, "There is a lot at stake."

This conversation about relevance seems to point to the existential question, do I matter? Framed from an evolutionary standpoint, the question relates to one of survival: does "do I matter" equate to an increased likelihood of survival? In this case, the survival is social—improving one's position in the pecking order, not being left out, or at least knowing where one stands in relation to others. When I was in middle school, seeking peer approval certainly felt like a life-or-death survival skill. The uncertainty of not knowing whether I was going to be accepted by a certain group was much more nerve-racking than simply being known, regardless of how popular the group was. Having clear feedback staves off the angsty questions that keep us from sleeping at night. As with the examples involving Facebook or Instagram, it may be that social survival can be meted out through the simple "rules" of reward-based learning, which were evolutionarily set up to help us remember where to find food. Each time we get a thumbs-up from our peers, we get that jolt of excitement and then learn to repeat the behaviors that led to the like. We have to eat to live; our social food may taste like real food to our brain, activating the same pathways.

Facebook Addiction Disorder

Returning to Danielle in the Louvre, let's say that after a bit of button pressing, she develops the habit of posting pictures to Facebook or Instagram. Like the teenagers in the *This American Life* podcast, she has learned that likes feel good. She is following Skinner's rules of positive reinforcement. So what happens when she doesn't feel good?

WOMAN (DRIVING HOME FROM WORK AND THINKING TO HER-
SELF): "Wow, today sucked."

WOMAN'S MIND (TRYING TO CHEER HER UP): "Sorry you don't
feel so good. You know, when you post pictures to Facebook,
you feel pretty good, right? Why don't you try that so you'll feel
better?"

WOMAN: "Great idea!" (checks her Facebook feed)

What is the problem here? It is the same learning process that
Skinner described, just with a different trigger. She is tapping into the
negative reinforcement side of the equation. Besides posting to feel
good, she is about to learn that she can do the same to make unpleasant feelings (such as sadness) go away—at least temporarily. The more
she does this, the more this behavior becomes reinforced—to the
point where it becomes automatic, habitual, and, yes, even addictive.

Though this scenario might sound simplistic, several key social
and technological advances now provide the conditions for the Inter-
net and technology overuse and addiction that are emerging today.
First, social media outlets such as YouTube, Facebook, and Instagram
lower the barriers for sharing something that is happening, virtually
anywhere, to almost nothing. Take a picture, tap "post," and you are
done. The name *Insta*gram says it all. Second, social media provide
the perfect forum for gossip, which in itself is rewarding. Third,
Internet-based social interaction is frequently asynchronous (not happening at the same time), which allows for selective and strategic
communication. To maximize the greatest likelihood of likes, we can
rehearse, rewrite, and take multiple photos before we post comments
or pictures. Here is an example from the *This American Life* podcast:

IRA GLASS (HOST): When a girl posts an unflattering selfie, or just a
selfie that makes her look uncool, other girls will take screenshots

to save the image and gossip about it later. Happens all the time. And so even though they're old hands at posting selfies—they've been posting since sixth grade—it can be nervous-making to post one. So they take precautions.

ELLA (TEENAGER): We all ask people before we post it, like, send in, like, a group chat, or, like, send to your friends, like, should I post this? Do I look pretty?

GLASS: And so it'd be like you run it by, like, four or five friends.

What are they describing? Quality control! They are testing to make sure the quality of their product (their image) meets industry standards before leaving the assembly line. If the aim is to get likes (positive reinforcement) and avoid people gossiping about them (negative reinforcement), they can do a test run before releasing their pictures to the public. Add to this mix the uncertainty of *when* or *whether* someone is going to post a comment to your picture. In behavioral psychology, this will-they-or-won't-they unpredictability is a feature of intermittent reinforcement—giving a reward only some of the time when a behavior is performed. Perhaps not surprisingly, this type of reinforcement schedule is the one that Las Vegas casinos use for their slot machines—pay out on a schedule that seems random but is just frequent enough to keep us in the game. By stirring all these ingredients together, Facebook came up with a winning recipe. Or at least one that gets us hooked. Put another way, this "glue" of intermittent reinforcement makes the whole thing sticky, or addictive. How sticky is it? A growing body of research provides some intriguing data.

In a study entitled "Hooked on Facebook," Roselyn Lee-Won and colleagues argued that the need for self-presentation—forming and maintaining positive impressions of ourselves on other people—

is "central to understanding the problematic use of online media."[6] The researchers showed that the need for social assurance was correlated with excessive and uncontrolled Facebook use, especially in people who perceive themselves as being deficient in social skills. When we are feeling anxious, bored, or lonely, we post an update, a callout of sorts to all our Facebook friends, who then respond by liking our post or writing a short comment. That feedback reassures us that we are connected, being paid attention to. In other words, we learn to go online or post something to our social media sites in order to get the reward that indicates we are relevant, we matter. Each time we are assured, we get reinforced, the loneliness is dissipated, and the connection feels good. We learn to come back for more.

So what happens when people get hooked on Facebook to make them feel better? In a 2012 study, Zach Lee and colleagues asked this question.[7] They looked to see whether the use of Facebook for mood regulation could explain deficient self-regulation of Facebook use itself (that is, Facebook Addiction Disorder). In other words, like a cocaine addict chasing a high, were people getting trapped in checking their Facebook feeds in an attempt to feel better? My patients who use cocaine don't feel great during their binges and definitely feel worse afterward. Analogously, Lee's research team found that a preference for online social interaction correlated with deficient mood regulation and *negative* outcomes such as a diminished sense of self-worth and increased social withdrawal. Let me say that again: online social interaction *increased* social withdrawal. People obsessively went on Facebook to feel better, yet afterward felt worse. Why? Just like learning to eat chocolate when we are sad, habitually going to social media sites doesn't fix the core problem that made us sad in the first place. We have simply learned to associate chocolate or Facebook with feeling better.

Worse yet, what can be rewarding for someone posting his or her latest and greatest pictures or pithy comments can be sad-making for others. In a study entitled "Seeing Everyone Else's Highlight Reels: How Facebook Usage Is Linked to Depressive Symptoms," Mai-Ly Steers and colleagues found evidence that Facebook users felt depressed when comparing themselves to others.[8] Duh. Despite the asynchronous nature of Facebook, which allows us to selectively post the best and brightest of ourselves, when we see *others* embellishing their lives—when we witness their perfectly framed "candid" shots, their extravagant vacations—we might not feel so good about our own lives. This unhappiness can be especially poignant as we look up from our computer screens and stare at the walls of our windowless cubicles right after being criticized by the boss. We think, "I want *their* life!" Like pressing hard on the gas pedal when the car is stuck in the snow (which only gets it more stuck), we spin out in our own habit loops, performing the same behaviors that brought those rewards previously, without realizing that doing so is making things worse. It isn't our fault—it is just how our brains work.

Mistaken Happiness

The phenomenal *what* of habit formation described in this chapter is familiar to all of us in one form or another, whether our vice is cocaine, cigarettes, chocolate, e-mail, Facebook, or whatever quirky habits we have learned over the years.

Now that we have a better sense of *how* habits get set up, and *why* these automatic processes are perpetuated—through positive and negative reinforcement—we can start looking at our lives to see how we might be driven by our habit loops. What levers are we pressing for reward?

As in the old joke (or dictum) about addiction, the first step to working on a problem is to admit that we have one. This isn't to say that every habit that we have is an addiction. It just means that we have to figure out which of our habits are causing that feeling of dis-ease and which aren't. Tying our shoes is probably not stress inducing. A compulsion to post a selfie in the middle of our own wedding ceremony is more a cause for concern. These extremes aside, we can start by examining what happiness actually feels like.

In his book *In This Very Life,* the Burmese meditation teacher Sayadaw U Pandita, wrote, "In their quest for happiness, people mistake excitement of the mind for real happiness."[9] We get excited when we hear good news, start a new relationship, or ride a roller coaster. Somewhere in human history, *we were conditioned to think that the feeling we get when dopamine fires in our brain equals happiness.* Don't forget, this was probably set up so that we would remember where food could be found, not to give us the feeling "you are now fulfilled." To be sure, defining happiness is a tricky business, and very subjective. Scientific definitions of happiness continue to be controversial and hotly debated. The emotion doesn't seem to be something that fits into a survival-of-the-fittest learning algorithm. But we can be reasonably sure that the anticipation of a reward isn't happiness.

Is it possible that we have become disoriented about the causes of our stress? We are constantly bombarded by advertising telling us that we aren't happy, but that we *can* be as soon as we buy this car or that watch, or get cosmetic surgery so that our selfies will always come out great. If we are stressed and see an ad for clothes (trigger), go to the mall and buy them (behavior), and come home and look in the mir-ror and feel a little better (reward), we may be training ourselves to perpetuate the cycle. What does this reward actually feel like? How long does the feeling last? Does it fix whatever caused our dis-ease in the first place, and presumably make us happier? My cocaine-dependent patients describe the feeling of getting high with terms like "edgy," "restless," "agitated," and even "paranoid." That doesn't sound like happiness to me (and they sure don't look happy). Indeed, we may be mindlessly pressing our dopamine levers, thinking that this is as good as it gets. Our stress compass may be miscalibrated, or we may not know how to read it. We may be mistakenly pointing ourselves toward these dopamine-driven rewards instead of away from them. We may be looking for love in all the wrong places.

Whether we are teenagers, baby boomers, or members of some generation in between, most of us use Facebook and other social media. Technology has remade the twenty-first-century economy, and while much of the innovation is beneficial, the uncertainty and volatility of tomorrow sets us up for learning that leads to addiction or other types of harmful behavior. Facebook, for example, knows what pushes our buttons, by expertly tracking which buttons we push, and it uses this information to keep us coming back for more. Does going on Facebook or using social media when I am sad make me feel better or worse? Isn't it time that we learn how to pay attention to what dis-ease and the reward of reinforcement learning feel like in our bodies and minds? If we stop the lever pressing long enough to step back and reflect on the actual rewards, we can start to see what behaviors orient us *toward* stress, and (re)discover what truly makes us happy. We can learn to read our compass.

3

Addicted to Ourselves

Ego, the self which he has believed himself to be, is nothing but a pattern of habits.

—*Alan Watts*

A confession: during a few summers of my MD-PhD program, I would sneak out of my lab rotations for a few hours and watch live coverage of the Tour de France instead of doing my work. Why? I was obsessed with Lance Armstrong. The Tour is considered one of, if not *the* most grueling endurance races of all time. Cyclists ride roughly 2,200 miles over the course of three weeks in July. Whoever finishes in the shortest total amount of time takes home the crown. To be victorious, a rider has to be able to win in all conditions: endurance, mountain climbs, and individual time trials, all while being the toughest mentally. To get back on your bike day after day, in all conditions, when your exhausted body is urging you to simply quit is really amazing.

Lance was unstoppable. After surviving metastatic testicular cancer, he won the 1999 Tour and then went on a tear—winning seven consecutive races (the former record was five wins). I still remember sitting in the dorm lounge (where there was a big-screen television) and cheering him through one of the mountain stages in

2003. He was in a pack of leaders racing down a steep descent when one of the riders ahead of him suddenly crashed. To avoid wrecking, he instinctively steered his bike *off the road,* down into a field, riding full speed through the uneven terrain before hopping his bike back onto the road and rejoining the group of leaders. I knew he had skills, but that move was unbelievable, and the British announcers said as much (announcer: "I've never seen anything like that in my life"). I was electrified for the rest of the day, and for years after would get the same excited feeling in my stomach when I replayed the scene in my head.

I got hooked on Lance. He spoke French at the press conferences after each stage of the race. He started a foundation to help people with cancer. And on and on. He could do no wrong. His unfolding journey was such an exciting story. Which was why I couldn't stay in the lab, dutifully doing my research and waiting to watch just the highlights of his racing. I had to be there to see what other amazing feat he was going to do in the next stage (and the next year). So when the doping allegations started surfacing, I vehemently defended him to anyone who would listen—including myself.

This story is a great example of subjective bias—mine in this case. I had developed the subjective bias that Lance was clearly the best cyclist ever. This bias led me to get caught up in the story. I couldn't let go of my idea that Lance couldn't possibly have doped, which caused me a fair amount of suffering. Remember: addiction can be broadly defined as repeated use despite adverse consequences. Was I addicted to Lance? And why couldn't I simply look at the facts as they began piling up? It turns out that these two questions may be related, and understanding this relationship may help shed light on how habits, and even addictions, are formed and maintained.

A Tale of Two Selves

Self #1: The Simulator

I first came across Prasanta Pal in the neuroimaging analysis computer cluster at Yale. A compact and soft-spoken gentleman with a ready smile, he had just received his PhD in applied physics. When we met, he was using fMRI to measure turbulence in blood flow through the heart's chambers. He had seen a paper of mine on brain activity during meditation, and over a cup of tea, he told me how he had grown up with meditation as part of his culture in India.[1] Prasanta was excited to see that it was being researched seriously. In fact, he was interested in joining my lab and putting his particular skills to use.

It was a good fit. Prasanta's area of expertise was in simulating data to optimize real-world systems. In my lab, he set up a number of Monte Carlo simulations—those that use random sampling methods to predict likely (probabilistic) outcomes in systems with many unknowns. Monte Carlo simulations run through numerous scenarios and, based on available information, suggest which ones would be most likely to happen if they were played out in real life. My brain had been doing a Monte Carlo simulation to keep Lance on a tall pedestal. Why had it gotten stuck?

Consider this: we may be doing something like Prasanta's simulations in our heads *all the time.* When we are driving on the highway and quickly approaching our exit, but are in the wrong lane, we start mentally simulating. We look at the distances between the cars, their relative speed, our speed, and how far it is to the exit, and we start mentally calculating whether we need to speed up to get in front of the car next to us or slow down to tuck in behind it. Another example: we receive an invitation to a party. We open it, scan to see who it is from and when the party will occur, and start *imagining ourselves at the party* to see who might be there, whether the food will be good, whether we will hurt the host's feelings if we don't attend, and what other things we could be doing instead (the bigger better offer). We might even do a verbal simulation with our spouse or partner as we talk over whether we should go or stay in and binge on Netflix movies.

These simulations come in handy daily. It is much better to mentally test a few scenarios instead of pulling out into traffic and causing an accident. And it is better to mentally rehearse the party's possibilities rather than to arrive at it and have that "oh crap" feeling wash over us as we walk through the door and see who is there.

At the lab, Prasanta worked to determine an ideal configuration of an EEG headset for measuring specific regional brain activity during our neurofeedback studies. He had to figure out how to reduce the number of data collection inputs recorded from the headset from 128 to 32, and so his simulations randomly removed one input at a time, from anywhere across the scalp. Imagine physically doing that much work. Monte Carlo simulations are tremendously helpful at efficiently solving complex problems.

Though nobody knows for sure, humans' capacity to mentally simulate probably evolved as agrarian societies emerged, increasing the need to plan for the future (for example, scheduling the planting of crops a certain amount of time before expecting to harvest them). In his book *The Curse of the Self,* Mark Leary wrote that around fifty thousand years ago, both agriculture and representational art arose—and so did boat making. Leary points out that just as it is helpful to plan when to plant based on harvest times, boat making is "a task that requires mentally imaging one's analogue— I will be using a boat at some later time."[2] Mental simulation is evolutionarily adaptive.

While our Stone Age ancestors may have planned, their planning focused on that season's harvest, the relatively short term. Fast-forward to the modern day. We live in a society that is much more sedentary—we are not hunting for food or living from one harvest to the next. We are also more long-term focused. Forget about the next harvest. We plan for college graduation, careers, and retirement—even colonizing Mars. And we have more time to sit around and think about ourselves, as if simulating the next chapter of our lives.

Several factors affect how well our mental simulations work, including their time frames and our interpretations of the data that we simulate. Simulating something far in the future decreases our accuracy because the number of unknown variables is huge. For example, trying to predict, as a sixth grader, where I will go to college is pretty hard compared to doing the same simulation while a senior in high school, when I know my high school grades and SAT scores, the schools I have applied to, and other pertinent information. As a sixth grader, I don't even know *what type* of college I may want to go to.

Perhaps even more importantly, the quality of our data and *how we interpret them* can skew the predictions that come out of our mental simulations. Subjective bias comes into play here—our viewing the world through our own glasses, seeing it the way we *want to* rather than perhaps how it actually is. Let's say we're juniors in high school, fired up after a recruiter from Princeton gives a presentation at our school, and we spend the rest of the day imagining ourselves as freshmen there, attending a capella concerts under the gothic arches, and trying out for the crew team. If we scored 1200 on our SATs, whereas the average score of students admitted to Princeton was 1450, it doesn't matter how great we, our friends, or our parents *think* we are. Unless we are headed for the Olympics or our parents donate a building (or two), the likelihood that we will be going to Princeton is pretty low, no matter how many simulations we do in our heads. Our subjective bias isn't going to make the world conform to our view of it—and can actually lead us down the wrong path when we act as if it will.

With this in mind, let's return to my view of Lance. Why was I so caught up in the story that he couldn't have doped, spinning my wheels on scenario after scenario? Had I been so blinded by subjective bias that my off-kilter simulations were all ending in a bust? Had I become addicted to my view of the world?

Let's look at some data:

1. *Lance had miraculously come back from cancer to win the king of all cycling races.* My interpretation: he was the perfect example of the "American dream." If you put your head down and do the work, you can accomplish anything. This was especially compelling to me, having grown up poor in Indiana, being told by my college counselor in high school that I would never get into Princeton, and so forth.

2. *He had a reputation for being a bit of a jerk.* My interpretation: he is competitive. Of course people are going to be jealous of his success and say bad things about him.

3. *He used performance-enhancing drugs.* My interpretation: the system was out to get him. It had been chasing him for years and couldn't prove a thing.

So when Lance broke down on an interview with Oprah Winfrey, admitting that he had doped (and even had developed and maintained an elaborate scheme to keep from being caught for *years*), my brain went into a tailspin. I wanted to view him a certain way—I was seeing him through my completely biased "he's amazing" glasses. The data were coming in loud and clear. I simply couldn't interpret them correctly. Not wanting to see the truth, I kept doing simulation after simulation to come up with an answer that fit my worldview. And his confession to Oprah smashed my subjective bias glasses—my Lance addiction ended. When I saw clearly what had happened, I sobered up quickly. I simply couldn't get excited about him anymore, even when recalling his past feats; my brain would remind me that he was superhuman at those moments because of his chemical helpers. And like my patients who learn to see clearly what they get from smoking, I lost my enchantment with Lance and became wiser about how my mind works in the process.

Our minds frequently create simulations to help optimize outcomes. These simulations can easily become skewed by subjective bias—seeing the world the way we want it to be rather than as it is. And the more that an erroneous viewpoint gets locked down in our minds, like a chemical addiction, the harder it is to see that we might have a problem, let alone change our behavior. In my case, learning the truth about Lance Armstrong was a humbling lesson about failing to stop and look at my stress compass—failing to look at the data and listen to my body and mind (the stress, endless simulations) to see whether I was missing something, instead being pulled along by my bias.

Self #2: The (Super)star of the Movie: Me!

As we saw in chapter 2, having a certain story in our heads can be pretty rewarding, perhaps to the point that we become addicted to our self-view. We lose flexibility in our thinking; we can no longer take in new information or adapt to our changing environment. We become the stars of our own movies, the center of the universe. This self-involvement often leads to negative outcomes down the road. I ate a lot of humble pie after the Armstrong story broke, which was relatively minor in the grand scheme of things—others were affected on a much larger scale (including the reputation of professional cyclists in general). And what happens when we as individuals, or as large groups of people, start to form a worldview about those who have the power to affect societies, such as politicians? Historically, this process was seen in the rise of charismatic world leaders such as Adolf Hitler. Modern politicians can become our personal Lance Armstrong—a great American success story that blinds us to reality.

How does this process of making me the center of the universe get set up?

A clue might come from a description of the ego by Alan Watts, a British-born American philosopher specializing in Eastern philosophies: "the self which he has believed himself to be."[3] Watts is pointing to the way that subjective bias gets set up and reinforced. We learn to view ourselves in a certain light over and over again until that image becomes a fixed view, a belief. This belief doesn't magically appear out of thin air. It develops with repetition. It is reinforced over time. We might start forming our sense of who we are and who we want to be as an adult in, say, our twenties, and then surround ourselves with people and situations that are likely to support our view of ourselves. This view gets strengthened as we go through the next few decades, getting better at what we do at work and at home until we're a fortysomething with a high-level job, a partner, property, family, and so forth.

Here is a metaphor that might help explain how these beliefs get set up. Let's say we go shopping for a new sweater or a winter coat. We bring a friend along for advice. We go to a boutique or a department store and start trying on clothes. How do we know what to buy? We look in the mirror to see what fits and also looks good. Then we ask our friend what she (or he) thinks. We might think a certain sweater is flattering, but aren't quite sure whether its quality is right or its price is too high. We go back and forth for fifteen minutes, not being able to make a decision. We look to our friend for help, and she says, "*Yes, that's it. You've got to get that one!*" So with this positive feedback, we head to the cash register.

Is the way we view *ourselves* shaped through the same lens of reward-based learning? For example, we might get an A on a test in sixth grade. We don't think much of it, but then get home and show it to our parents, who exclaim, "Great job! Look how smart you are!" This parental praise is rewarding—it feels good. We ace another test, and having gotten a hint from what happened the last time, hand it to our parents, expecting more praise, and receive it accordingly. With this reinforcement as motivation, we might make sure we study extra hard for the rest of the semester, and we get straight As on our report card. Over time, with our grades, friends, and parents telling us over and over that we are smart, we might start to believe it. After all, there is nothing to suggest otherwise.

It is the same with the shopping analogy. We have studied ourselves wearing the sweater in a three-way mirror, and been validated by our shopping buddy—we have gotten enough reassurance that it looks great. So why not wear it? When we try the same sweater on again and again, our brains can run simulations and start to predict the outcome: We will be stylish. We will be intelligent. We will be praised.

Over time, as the outcomes all come out the same, we get used to it. We become habituated to the reinforcement.

In a series of experiments in the 1990s, Wolfram Schultz demonstrated how this type of reinforcement learning and habituation ties in with dopamine. When recording the reward centers of monkey brains, he discovered that when they received juice as a reward in a learning task, dopamine neurons increased their firing rate during the initial learning periods, but decreased progressively over time, switching to a more steady-state, habitual mode of firing.[4] In other words, we learn that we are smart via a spritz of dopamine that feels good when we get praised. Yet when our parents say for the hundredth time, "Great job on getting straight As," we roll our eyes because we have become habituated to it—we believe them when they say we are smart, but the reward has lost its juice. As Watts pointed out, perhaps this view of being smart, over time, becomes "nothing but a pattern of habits." Like smoking or posting pithy quotes on Facebook, forming a view of ourselves such as "I'm the smart guy" can be rewarded and reinforced. We can also consider whether this process underlies other subjective biases—personality traits and characteristics that we carry around from day to day based on how we view ourselves, and thus color our worldview—our habits of self.

Pathological Personalities

We can start by exploring the extremes of the personality spectrum to see whether reward-based learning applies. Personality disorders are often described as maladaptive extensions of the same traits that describe normal personality, so they can be helpful in giving insight into the human condition. Think of it as taking a certain personality characteristic and amping it up tenfold. If we make it bigger, it becomes easier to see what is going on. Like addictions, these are behaviors that are repeated over and over to the point that they stand out in "normal society" because they are associated with negative consequences.

Let's take the premise that a normal self-view lies somewhere in the middle of the personality spectrum. Development of such a self-view would suggest that our childhood progressed over a more or less stable trajectory. From a reward-based-learning perspective, it would mean that our parents treated us somewhat predictably. If we got good grades, we were praised. If we lied or stole something, we were punished. And throughout our formative years, we received plenty of attention and love from our parents. They picked us up when we fell and hurt ourselves, reassuring us that we were smart (or as the teenage girls in chapter 2 put it, "relevant") when our friends shunned us at school. Over time, we developed a stable sense of self.

Consider someone who falls at one end of the spectrum, perhaps someone who has experienced too much ego boosting—someone who is arrogant or overly full of himself. For example, a former colleague of mine was seen as a "golden child" during residency training and early in his career. Whenever I ran into him, the topic of conversation was him. I got to hear about the papers he had published, the grants he was awarded (against stiff competition!), and his patients' excellent progress. I would congratulate him on his success, which would then prompt him to repeat this process the next time we ran into each other. Trigger (seeing Jud), behavior (success update), reward (being congratulated). What was I supposed to do? Tell him he was insufferable?

At the extreme of this spectrum lies what is called narcissistic personality disorder (NPD). NPD is characterized by goal setting based on gaining approval from others, excessive attunement to others' reactions (but only if they are perceived as relevant to self), excessive attempts to be the focus of attention, and admiration seeking. The cause of NPD is unclear, though it is likely that genetic factors play a role to some extent.[5] Seen from a simple (and probably simplistic) reward-based-learning perspective, we can imagine the "I'm smart" paradigm gone awry. Perhaps with the help of runaway parenting styles in which praise exceeds what is warranted ("Everyone gets a trophy, especially *you!*") and corrective punishment is nonexistent ("My child is on her own journey"), the reward-based learning process gets overly stimulated and cemented to a degree exceeding societal norms. Like someone who is genetically predisposed to getting hooked on alcohol, the child now has a taste—no, a need—for praise that cannot easily be sated. Instead of spirits, he needs ongoing positive reinforcement: "Like me, tell me I'm great, do it again."

Let's move to the other end of the spectrum. What happens when we don't develop a stable sense of self, whether normal or excessive? This deficiency may be the case with borderline personality disorder (BPD), which is characterized by the most recent *Diagnostic and Statistical Manual of Mental Disorders* (*DSM*) by a range of symptoms including "poorly developed or unstable self-image," "chronic feelings of emptiness," "intense, unstable, and conflicted close relationships, marked by mistrust, neediness, and anxious preoccupation with real or imagined abandonment," "fears of rejection by and/or separation from significant others," and "feelings of inferior self-worth."

During my psychiatric residency training, when I was learning about BPD, this list of symptom characteristics was difficult to understand. And we can see why. I couldn't hold all these seemingly loosely related symptoms together; they lacked consistency or coherence (at least in my mind). When patients came into my clinic or our psychiatric emergency room, I would pull out my list of criteria and see whether the "sweater" of BPD fit. It fit some better than others. Our medication options didn't help clue me in much, either, when trying to bring this symptom cluster together. The treatment guidelines suggested symptomatic relief: if they were depressed, we should treat their depression. If they showed up looking slightly psychotic (a "mini-psychotic episode"), prescribe them a low-dose antipsychotic. Yet these episodic treatments didn't have a great track record of helping people with BPD. Personality disorders are chronic and difficult to treat. In medical school, I learned that one of the "soft signs" (something akin to folklore that helps with a diagnosis but never makes it into the chart) of a BPD sufferer was someone who brought a teddy bear with him to the hospital. How could we treat adults with BPD, who in some sense had never grown up to form a stable self-image or identity?

I was handed down clinical wisdom from my mentors with a knowing wink of "Good luck, soldier!" as if I was going into battle and they were seasoned generals. Their advice included the following admonitions: "make sure you keep the same appointment time every week with them," "keep everything in your office the same," "if they call, begging for an extra appointment, be polite, but above all *don't* give it to them." "They will keep pushing and pushing your boundaries," I was warned. "Don't let them!" After working with a few patients with BPD, I started to see what my mentors were talking about. If I took a call from a frantic patient, I would get more (and more) calls. If I let a session run long, at the end of my next session there would be an angling for more time. My BPD patients took a disproportionate amount of my time and energy. I felt as if I were dodging bullets with each interaction. This *was* a battle. And one that I felt as though I was losing. I tried my best to hunker down and hold the line—no extra time, no extra appointments. Hold the line!

One day, after pondering an interaction for way too long (I was getting caught up, but didn't know it), something clicked. A lightbulb flicked on. I wondered: what happens if we don't have a stable upbringing? I started to look at BPD through the lens of operant conditioning. What if, instead of the steady stream of predictable feedback, someone with BPD had a childhood more like a slot machine, receiving intermittent instead of stable reinforcement? I did some research. Some of the most consistent findings related to childhood upbringing in people with BPD include low maternal affection as well as sexual and physical abuse.[6] My patients corroborated this. Plenty of neglect and abuse. What type of neglect? When I delved more deeply, they described their parents as being warm and loving sometimes. At other times they weren't—quite the opposite. *And they couldn't predict when mom or dad would come home looking to hug or hit them.* The pieces of the puzzle started to fit. Then the picture suddenly came together while I was standing at my whiteboard pondering someone's behavior from a recent interaction.

My patients' symptoms *and* my mentors' advice began to make sense. Someone with BPD may not have developed a stable sense of self, because *there were no predictable rules of engagement.* Worse than my addiction to Lance (at least his confession shut my simulations down for good), their brains were constantly in simulation overdrive, trying to figure out how to consistently feel loved, or at least alive. Like rats pressing levers or people posting on Facebook, they were unconsciously seeking ways to engineer that next dopamine hit. If my session went long, they felt special. Behavior. Reward. If I scheduled an extra session with them because they "really needed it," they felt special. Behavior. Reward. Naively, I never knew when they would be in a "crisis," and thus I had to decide on the fly how best to respond— and so neither my patients nor I could predict how I would behave. In the most basic sense, they wanted someone (in this case, me) to love them, to provide a stable attachment, a predictable roadmap of their world. Subconsciously, they were trying to trigger any behavior of mine that would indicate this. And if any of my behaviors were inconsistent, they would get the stickiest type of reinforcement. Unknowingly, I was providing the glue.

Looking through this new lens of reward-based learning, I could more easily understand my patients' perspectives. I could even empathize with them. For example, one of the hallmark (and formerly confusing) features of BPD is extreme idealization and devaluation of relationships. A paradox? One day they would talk about how great a new friendship or romantic relationship was, and then a few weeks later, that person would be on their "shit list." Looking for stability in their lives, they would throw everything they had into a blossoming relationship, which was likely rewarding for both sides—everyone likes attention. This positive feeling would wear off a bit for the other person as he (let's say) became habituated. The excessive attention from the BPD partner would at some point wake him up to what was happening, and he would start feeling a bit smothered. Wondering whether this preoccupation was healthy, he would back off a bit. My patient, sensing some instability, would go into overdrive: oh no, you are about to lose another one, give it everything you have! Which would backfire because it was the opposite of what was called for, leading to a breakup and another call for a special session to deal with yet another crisis. Triggered by feeling abandoned by her father, one of my patients has cycled through *close to a hundred* jobs and relationships as she desperately seeks security.

Now, instead of simply trying to dodge bullets and make it through another session with a patient, I could start asking relevant questions. Instead of trying to read a cryptic and seemingly ever-changing treatment manual, I imagined myself in a patient's shoes, feeling constantly out of sorts, looking for that next dopamine hit that would give me temporary relief. We could get right to the heart of the matter. I stopped feeling conflicted and guilty about not giving my BPD patients "extra" time, because I could clearly see that it would be more harmful than helpful, and my Hippocratic oath was pretty clear on this front: first do no harm. As I applied this framework and learned from it, treating patients with BPD became easier. I could help them learn to develop a more stable sense of themselves and their world, starting with the very simple guideline of always beginning and ending sessions on time—no more intermittent reinforcement—and with it would come stable learning and habituation. This technique seems ridiculously simple, yet it was surprisingly effective. I was no longer on the front lines fighting the "enemy." My treatment and my patients' outcomes both improved. I collaborated with my patients, not merely to manage their symptoms, but also to best help them live better lives. We had moved from applying Band-Aids to putting direct pressure on their wounds to stop the bleeding.

Returning to the concept of subjective bias: it was entirely possible that I was fooling myself in thinking that I was doing a great job with my patients. They might have been giving me positive reinforcement through their behavior—in this case, not firing me and looking for another doctor—in an attempt to please me (rewarding for both of us). To make sure that I wasn't simply swapping one glue for another, I talked to colleagues and gave lectures about framing BPD from a reward-based-learning standpoint (scientists and clinicians are great at pointing out errors in theories and treatments). This approach didn't seem crazy to them. When I discussed patients in case-based learning formats with residents, they thanked me for helping pull them back from the front lines, because they were doing a better job of understanding and, thus, treating their patients. And an intrepid chief resident, a few research colleagues, and I published a peer-reviewed paper (the holy grail for getting ideas into the broader field) entitled "A Computational Account of Borderline Personality Disorder: Impaired Predictive Learning about Self and Others through Bodily Simulation."[7]

In our paper, we argued for an algorithmic explanation of BPD symptoms that might be "a useful therapeutic guide toward treatments that addressed underlying pathophysiology." Seeing that BPD followed predictable rules, we could develop treatments for it. From this framework, we could more accurately than before pinpoint the core causes of, and contributing factors to, BPD. For example, altered reward-based learning could lead to significantly altered subjective bias in people with BPD. Just as I failed to accept Lance's doping despite clear evidence staring me in the face, people with BPD, especially when emotionally dysregulated, may often incorrectly interpret actions and outcomes (theirs and others'). This bias results in a failure to accurately simulate mental states (both those of others and their own). This psychological barrier can, for instance, explain the lavish attention that they bestow on others when starting a relationship; the intense interest seems justified to them but completely blown out of proportion or even creepy to others. And then what happens when their partner in a romantic relationship starts pulling back? If my baseline framework is that I want love (attention), I assume that the other person wants this as well, and I give her more love instead of stepping back to see what is real and accurate from her perspective— namely, that she may be feeling smothered. In other words, people with BPD may have difficulty with reward-based learning, and therefore may likewise have trouble predicting outcomes of interpersonal interactions. As in addictions in which drug seeking occupies much of one's time and mental space, people who carry a BPD diagnosis may be unknowingly angling for attention as a way to fill a deep feeling of emptiness, one short-acting dopamine hit at a time.

As we saw earlier, this type of learning failure leads to no good. It wastes energy and causes us to miss the mark when seeking stability in relationships and life in general. Multiply this tendency tenfold, and the results are personality traits that fall in the range of the pathological, including emotional lability (that is, frequent crises that, to the patient, genuinely feel like the end of the world), another hallmark feature of BPD. People with BPD get strung out and exhausted from the constant and frantic seeking. All this from a simple learning process gone awry.

A Return to the Middle

This view of reward-based learning extremes in personality, whether resulting in too little or too much self, can help us better understand and make sense of the human condition. Knowing that we mentally simulate (all the time) can be helpful. We can use this information to *become aware* of our simulations so that we don't get lost or caught up in them as often, saving time and energy.

An understanding of how subjective bias works can help us get simulations back on track when they go off course. And now we should be able to see more clearly where subjective bias can come from, namely, from somewhere on the spectrum between the "look how great I am" star of the movie and the shunned actress sitting backstage and plotting how to get in front of the camera. Seeking attention, reinforcement, or any other type of adoration can get us sucked into this addictive spectrum, which is fueled by our subjective bias and then feeds back into it. Simply seeing where we might be biased can start the process of taking off the glasses distorting our worldviews. Grasping how and when our subjective biases are out of whack can be the first step in updating them.

As mentioned earlier, being able to use information about subjective bias to improve our own lives starts with pulling out our stress compass so that we can clearly see the results of our actions. In chapter 2, we learned some of the ways that social media provide the glue to get us stuck on ourselves. Yet technology is just tapping into what we have been doing as social creatures for millennia. For example, what does it feel like at the exact moment someone flatters us? Does that warm glow have elements of excitement? Do we lean in and look for more? And what happens when we continually stroke someone else's ego, as I had unknowingly done with my colleague? What does he or she get, and what do we get out of it? I was certainly punished by having to listen to Mr. Wonderful over and over because of my ignorance.

Seeing situations such as these more clearly can help us step back and check our compass—are we perpetuating dis-ease (our own and others'), either habitually or because it seems like the easiest thing to do in the moment? If we step back and look carefully to see whether we are failing to read the compass correctly because of our own assumptions and biases, does this realization help us find a better way to proceed, one that might stop fueling the ego fires? Sometimes the situations and opportunities for improvement are not obvious, because we are so habituated to them. In his novel *Hocus Pocus,* Kurt Vonnegut wrote, "Just because we think we're so wonderful doesn't mean we really are." It can be helpful to become more aware of, and even challenge, our own views of ourselves. Sometimes flaws or strengths need to be pointed out to us, and our task is to learn to thank the messenger and take the feedback graciously—instead of shrinking away from constructive criticism or, at the other end of the spectrum, being unable to take a genuine compliment. Feedback is how we learn. At other times we can learn how best to (graciously) point this out to others, or at least start by putting up a sign in our mind: "Warning! Do not feed the egos."

4

Addicted to Distraction

Clever gimmicks of mass distraction yield a cheap soulcraft of addicted and self-medicated narcissists.

—*Cornel West*

Teenagers talk about the idea of having each other's "full attention." They grew up in a culture of distraction. They remember their parents were on cell phones when they were pushed on swings as toddlers. Now, their parents text at the dinner table and don't look up from their BlackBerry when they come for end-of-school day pickup.

—*Sherry Turkle*

Have you pulled up to a stoplight at night and looked into the cars around you, only to see others staring down at an eerie bluish-whitish light emanating from their crotches? Have you found yourself at work, in the middle of a project, suddenly have an urge to check your e-mail (again)?

Every month or so it seems, I see yet another opinion piece in the *New York Times* (my vice) written by someone addicted to technology. These read more like confessionals. They can't get any work done. Their personal lives are in shambles. What to do? They take a technology "fast" or "holiday," and after a few weeks, voilà! They are able to read more than a paragraph at a time in the novel they have had on their bedside table for the past year. Is it really that bad?

Let's see for ourselves, with the help of this short quiz. In this case, "X" is your cell phone usage. Put a checkmark in each box that applies to you.

☐ Using X for longer than you meant to
☐ Wanting to cut down or stop using X but not managing to
☐ Spending a lot of time using, or recovering from using, X
☐ Cravings and urges to use X
☐ Not managing to do what you should at work, home, or school because of X
☐ Continuing to use X even when it causes problems in relationships
☐ Giving up important social, occupational, or recreational activities because of X
☐ Using X again and again, even when it puts you in danger
☐ Continuing to use X even when you know you have a physical or psychological problem that could have been caused or made worse by it
☐ Needing more of X to get the effect you want (tolerance)
☐ Developing withdrawal symptoms that can be relieved by using X more.

Give yourself a point for each checkmark. The total number can help gauge whether your smartphone addiction is mild (2–3 checkmarks), moderate (4–5), or severe (6–7).

Remember the definition of addiction from chapter 1: "continued use, despite adverse consequences." The above quiz is actually a diagnostic checklist in the *DSM* that my colleagues and I use to determine whether someone has substance use disorder, and if so, how strong his or her addiction is.

How did you do? Like *half* the respondents to a 2016 Gallup poll who reported checking their phones several times an hour or more often, did you think, "*Whew,* I'm just mildly addicted. No big deal." Or perhaps, "Cell phone addiction is a victimless crime, right?"

No matter what you are thinking right now, can we at least agree that keeping our children safe falls into the category of "major obligations"? Good. Ben Worthen, in a *Wall Street Journal* article in 2012, wrote that childhood injury rates have declined steadily since the 1970s, thanks to basic improvements in playgrounds, the installation of baby gates, and the like.[1] Yet according to the Centers for Disease Control and Prevention (CDC), nonfatal injuries to children less than five years of age *increased* 12 percent between 2007 and 2010. The iPhone was released in 2007, and by 2010 the number of Americans who owned a smartphone had increased sixfold. Was this a coincidence? Remember: our brains love to make associations between things—and correlation does not mean causation.

In 2014, Craig Palsson published a paper entitled "That Smarts! Smartphones and Child Injuries."[2] He pulled data from the CDC about nonfatal, unintentional injuries to children under five between the years 2007 and 2012. He then cleverly surmised that because the iPhone was at that time available only through AT&T, since its 3G network had expanded its coverage, he could use these data to determine whether increased iPhone use indirectly played a causal role in the spike in childhood injuries. Based on a national hospital injury surveillance database, he could tell whether a hospital that reported a childhood injury was "located in an area with access to 3G at the time of injury." He found just that: injuries to children under five (those most at risk in the absence of parental supervision) increased when areas began getting 3G service, suggesting an indirect yet causal relationship between injury and smartphone use. Not definitive proof, but well worthy of more investigation.

Worthen's *Wall Street Journal* article highlighted an instance when a man was walking with his eighteen-month-old son and texting his wife at the same time. He looked up to see that his son had wandered off into the middle of a domestic dispute being broken up by a policeman, and the boy "almost got trampled" by the policeman.

We read stories and see YouTube videos about people who, distracted by their smartphones, walk into traffic and off piers into the ocean. Perhaps not surprisingly, a report in 2013 found that pedestrian injuries related to cell phone use more than tripled between 2007 and 2010.[3] And in the first six months of 2015, pedestrian fatalities increased 10 percent, the largest spike in four decades, according to the report.[4] A few years ago, the city of New Haven spray-painted "LOOK UP" in big yellow letters at crosswalks around the Yale University campus (New York City has taken similar measures). Are admission standards lower these days (probably not), or are these young adults forgetting simple survival skills, overpowered by the pull of their phones?

How Did We Get So Distracted?

Since reward-based learning has engendered a selective survival advantage, namely, we learn to remember where to find food and to avoid danger, how is it that technology seems to be doing the opposite—endangering us? In chapter 2, I outlined how certain technological factors provide opportunities for reward-based learning related to ourselves (instant access, rapid reward, and so forth).

In chapter 3, I briefly mentioned that Wolfram Schultz led a series of groundbreaking experiments showing that when monkeys get a reward (a bit of juice) for a behavior, their nucleus accumbens gets a spritz of dopamine. The reaction of neurons to this spritz of dopamine is termed "phasic firing" because it doesn't happen continuously. Over time, dopamine-activated neurons stop this type of firing, returning to a low level of continuous (in the lingo: tonic) activation when a reward is received. As currently understood in neuroscience, phasic firing helps us learn to pair a behavior with a reward.

This is where the magic happens. Once behavior and reward are paired, the dopamine neurons change their phasic firing pattern to respond to stimuli that *predict* rewards. Enter the trigger into the scene of reward-based learning. We see someone smoking a cigarette, and we suddenly get a craving. We smell fresh-baked cookies, and our mouths start watering in anticipation. We see someone who yelled at us recently approaching us, and we immediately start looking for an escape route. These are simply environmental cues that we have learned to pair with rewarding behavior. After all, we haven't eaten the cookie or engaged the enemy. Our brains are *predicting* what will happen next. I see this with my patients, fidgeting and squirming as they anticipate their next hit of whatever they are addicted to. Sometimes they get a little triggered in my office, simply by recalling their last relapse. The memory is enough to get their dopamine flowing. Watching a movie that involves drug use can move them into drug-seeking mode until that itch is scratched by using—if they don't have the mental tools to ride the wave of craving.

Interestingly, these dopamine neurons not only go into prediction mode when we are triggered, but also fire when an *unpredicted* reward is received. This might sound confusing. Why would our brains fire both when predicting a reward and when something un-predicted happens? Let's return to the "I'm smart" example from chapter 3. If we come home from school for the first time with an A on an exam, we don't know how our parents will respond, because we have never been in that scenario before. We carefully hand our paper to our parents, wondering what is going to happen next. Our brains don't know what to predict, because this is new territory. The first time our parents praise us, we get a big phasic release of dopamine in our brain, which subsequently sets off the whole reward-based learn-ing and habituation process discussed earlier. The same thing happens the first time we bring home a C (what will they think!?), and so on until we map out much of our everyday world. If my best friend, Suzy, knocks on the door for a playdate, I anticipate good times ahead. If she comes in the house and suddenly unleashes a tirade about what a terrible friend I am, my dopamine system, not having seen that one coming, goes berserk. The next time I see Suzy, I might be a little more guarded or on the lookout, since I am less certain about what our interaction will be. We can see how this might confer a survival advantage: it is helpful to be able to predict whom we can and can't trust. Broadly speaking, it is important that we have the neural tools to build a reservoir of trust.

What does any of this have to do with being distracted by smart-phones? What we know about reward-based learning begins to ex-plain how we get sucked into abnormal—or dare I say, addictive—technology use. Knowing that anticipation gets our dopamine flowing, businesses use this to get us to click on their ads or apps. For a nice example of anticipation, here are three consecutive headlines from the front page of CNN's website: "Star Wars Stormtroopers: What's Their Message?," "Affluenza Teen: The Damage He Caused," and "Why Putin Praised Trump." These are written not as fact-based messages, such as Putin praises Trump for being "lively" and "talented," but instead as teasers to get our anticipation juices flowing—to get us fired up, and our dopamine neurons firing, so that we will click the link to read the article. No wonder they call such attention grabbers "clickbait."

What about e-mail and texting? Our computers and phones offer services so that we can get alerts each time we get an e-mail—push notifications. How nice! We certainly don't want to miss that "important" e-mail from the boss do we? Instant message? Even better. Now I don't even have to spend any extra time opening the e-mail—the message is right there. Twitter? A tweet's 140-character limit is not magic. That length was specifically chosen because we will *automatically* read a message that size. And this is where unpredictability comes in: each time we *unexpectedly* hear the bell, beep, or chirp, our brains fire off a shot of dopamine. As mentioned in earlier chapters, intermittent reinforcement leads to the strongest, stickiest type of learning. By turning on our e-mail and text alerts in order to be more available and responsive, we have set ourselves up much like Pavlov's dogs, which were trained to salivate in anticipation of receiving food when they heard him ring the bell.

Let me be clear. This section on the potential dangers of communication technology is not the rant of a Luddite. I prefer e-mail to the Pony Express or carrier pigeons. Often, a text can answer a question more quickly than a phone call. These things can make our lives more efficient and potentially more productive. I am bringing together how our brains learn and what our current technology is set up to do so that we can develop a clearer picture of where our distracted behavior comes from. Let's now tie that information together with what we know about mental simulations.

Simulations Gone Wild

In chapter 3, we talked about the evolution of mental simulations as ways to anticipate potential outcomes so that we can make better decisions when there are multiple variables at play. If we are subjectively biased—seeing the world as we want or expect it to be—these simulations don't work so well. They keep trying to come up with "the right" solution, or at least ones that fit somewhere within our worldview. It can certainly be rewarding to simulate how best to approach our boss for a raise and then to have the meeting go just as anticipated. Yet in some instances these same types of simulations get hijacked by our reward system, leading us to spend time "elsewhere" when we should be watching our children or doing the work that will get us that raise. Yes, I am talking about daydreaming.

Daydreaming is a great example of our attention being diverted from the task at hand. Let's say we are sitting on the sidelines at our child's soccer practice. All the kids are down at the other end of the field; nothing particularly exciting is happening. A thought pops up about the family vacation scheduled for next month, and suddenly we are planning for the trip or imagining ourselves sitting in the warm sand, ocean breezes blowing, decked out with our favorite book and a refreshing drink while the kids play in the water (yes, we are watching them!). One moment we are at soccer practice, and the next we are a thousand miles away.

What is wrong with daydreaming? Absolutely nothing, right? If we find ourselves in a planning daydream, we are multitasking, getting some needed work done. If we end up on the beach, maybe we are getting some mental vitamin D from the simulated sun. It sure does feel good!

What are we missing? Let's unpack the example of making that mental "to do" list as we plan for a vacation or some other future event. We make the list in our head. Doing so might lead to another thought such as "Gosh, I've got a lot to do to plan for this trip!" or "I hope I didn't forget anything." We eventually wake up from the daydream and return to soccer practice. We didn't actually make the list, because the trip is far off, so we repeat the process the next week. From the perspective of orienting to stress, does this mental simulation move us away from our dis-ease? On average, no. It can actually make things worse.

In 2010, Matt Killingsworth and Dan Gilbert investigated what happens when our minds wander or daydream (in the lingo: stimulus-independent thought).[5] Using iPhones, they randomly prompted over 2,200 people to answer a few questions as they went about their day. They asked, "What are you doing right now?" "Are you thinking about something other than what you are currently doing," and "How are you feeling right now?" (response choices ranged from "very bad" to "very good"). How much do you think people reported daydreaming? Ready for this? They found that *almost 50 percent of the time,* people reported that they were off task. That is half of waking life! Here is a key, counterintuitive finding: when the researchers correlated happiness with being on or off task, people reported *being less happy,* on average, when their minds were wandering. The study concluded, "A human mind is a wandering mind, and a wandering mind is an unhappy mind."

How can this be? Thinking about Hawaii feels good—remember that dopamine spritz when we anticipate future behavior? And on average, daydreaming about pleasant events was rated at the same level of happiness as being on task in the moment—no matter what the task was. But taken together with all the neutral and unpleasant mind wandering, which, not surprisingly, was reported as being correlated with lower happiness scores, we get the "unhappy mind" conclusion that Killingsworth and Gilbert put forth. How many song lyrics and sayings have we seen about life happening while we're busy making other plans? We might be not only working ourselves up into a state of needless worry or excitement when we daydream, but also missing the soccer game.

So it seems that our brains are wired to form associations between feelings and events—for example, Hawaii is nice. We get "rewarded" in a dopamine sense, too, for anticipating future events. Trouble arises when these come together: not having much (if any) control over what type of thoughts we have—pleasant or unpleasant—we end up getting swept away in daydreams of delight and disaster, distracted from what is right in front of our face, whether it is a car bearing down on us or our child's first goal. What can we do?

Good Old-Fashioned Self-Control (Or Not)

The beloved film *Chocolat* (2000) is set in a quaint and quiet town in France during the season of Lent. The pious townsfolk spend lots of time in church listening to sermons intended to make them feel guilty about their "sinful" ways even as they give up daily vices—such as chocolate. Enter our heroine, Vianne, played by Juliette Binoche, blown in by the north wind and wearing a hooded red cape (the devil!). She sets up a *chocolaterie,* and all hell breaks loose. Using chocolate as the scapegoat, the rest of the movie pits righteous self-control against sinful indulgence.

Chocolat is everyone's story. Each of us has a guilty pleasure—an excess, a vice—that we manage to control on our best days. If we have an urge to pull out our smartphone to check e-mail at our kid's soccer practice, that pious angel voice in our head chimes in, "Oh, you know you should be watching your child." Or if we are driving, hear the beep of a new text message, and get antsy to see who it's from, she reminds us, "Remember what you heard on the radio: texting behind the wheel is more dangerous than drunk driving!" We thank our better angels for helping us to stay involved in our children's lives, and to not be the cause of an accident on the highway.

You are already familiar with what we are doing when we listen to the angel—practicing good old-fashioned self-control. Scientists call this cognitive control: we use *cognition* to *control* our behavior. Treatments such as cognitive behavioral therapy apply this kind of control to a range of disorders, including depression and addiction. Some people, like my good friend Emily, are natural models of cognitive control. After the birth of her first child, she was thirty pounds heavier than her pre-pregnancy weight. To get back to her previous weight, she calculated the number of calories she would have to restrict each day to lose those pounds in five months. She simply rationed her calorie allowance over the course of each day (including adjustments for exercise) to stay within her daily limit. Bada bing, bada boom: back to her pre-pregnancy weight as planned. And she did this again with her second child: fifteen pounds in two months.

For those of us who are screaming, "That's not fair!" or "I tried that and failed," Emily, besides being wonderful in many ways, has the mind of Mr. Spock from *Star Trek* when it comes to self-control. By this, I mean that she has a very logical mind, reasons things out, and executes without getting caught up in the emotion-laden stories that often plague us: *that's too hard, I can't do that.* Mr. Spock was famous for helping Captain Kirk calm down when he got emotionally worked up over something. When Kirk was about to steer the *Enterprise* into a seemingly disastrous scenario, Spock would look at him expressionlessly and remark, "Highly illogical, Captain." And Emily would simply cool her "but I'm hungry" jets and wait until the next day, when her daily calorie allowance would be up again.

Neuroscientists are beginning to uncover the brain correlates that represent the balance between Mr. Spock, our rational mind, and Captain Kirk, our passionate and sometimes irrational mind. In fact, Daniel Kahneman (author of *Thinking, Fast and Slow*) won a 2002 Nobel Prize in Economics for his work in this area. Kahneman and others describe these two ways of thinking as System 1 and System 2.

System 1 represents the more primitive, emotional system. Like Captain Kirk, it reacts quickly, based on impulse and emotion. Brain regions associated with this system include midline structures such as the medial (meaning: situated in the middle) prefrontal cortex and the posterior cingulate cortex. These areas are consistently activated when something related to us happens, such as thinking about ourselves, daydreaming, or craving something.[6] System 1 represents the "I want" urges and impulses as well as gut instincts (instant impressions). Kahneman calls this "fast" thinking.

System 2, which is the part of the brain that most recently evolved, represents our higher capacities, those that make us uniquely human. These functions include planning, logical reasoning, and self-control.

System 1: the medial prefrontal cortex (*left*) and posterior cingulate cortex (right), midline brain structures that are part of a system of brain regions involved in self-referential, impulsive reaction.

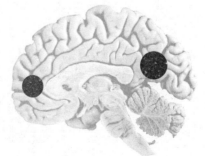

Brain regions in this system include the dorsolateral prefrontal cortex.[7] If the Vulcan brain is comparable to its human counterpart, Mr. Spock's dorsolateral prefrontal cortex functions like a freight train—slow and steady, keeping him on track. We can think of "slow" System 2 as representing "it's not about me—do what needs to be done" types of thoughts.

Chocolat's comte de Reynaud, the town's beloved mayor, is a model of self-control, restraining himself from enjoying delicious food (croissants, tea, and coffee—he drinks hot lemon water) or having unwanted thoughts about his secretary, Caroline. My friend Emily and Mr. Spock would be proud! As the movie progresses, he and his self-control confront bigger and bigger challenges. Sometimes it is an obvious struggle, but he always powers through, sweating and gritting his teeth.

The night before Easter, the comte is devastated by seeing Caroline, another model of self-control, leave the *chocolaterie*. Convinced that Vianne and her chocolate are ruining his model town, he loses his composure, breaks into her store, and begins destroying the hedonistic and decadent creations in her window display. In the fray, a bit of chocolate cream lands on his lips. After tasting it, he snaps and, depleted of all self-restraint, falls into a feeding frenzy. Although few of us pillage chocolate shops, how many have polished off an entire pint of our favorite ice cream?

Dorsolateral prefrontal cortex

System 2: the dorsolateral prefrontal cortex, a lateral brain structure involved in cognitive control.

What happened to the mayor (and the rest of us who aren't Emily or Mr. Spock)? As the youngest member of the brain, System 2 is just like any new member of a group or organization—it has the weakest voice. So when we get stressed or run out of gas, guess which part of the brain is the first to bail? System 2. Amy Arnsten, a neuroscientist at Yale, put it this way: "Even quite mild acute uncontrollable stress can cause a rapid and dramatic loss of prefrontal cognitive abilities."[8] In other words, it doesn't take much in our everyday lives to send us off the rails.

The psychologist Roy Baumeister refers to this stress reaction, perhaps ironically, as "ego depletion." Recent work has supported the idea that just like a car with only enough gas in the tank to keep going, we may have only enough gas in our self-control tank for any one day. Specifically, his group has found that across a number of different types of behavior, "resource depletion" (that is, running out of gas in the tank) directly affected the likelihood of someone being able to resist a desire.

In one study, Baumeister's research team used smartphones to track people's behavior and their degree of desire for a number of temptations, including social contact and sex.[9] The phone would randomly ask them whether they were currently having a desire, or had had one in the past thirty minutes. Participants then rated the desire's strength, whether it interfered with other goals, and whether they were able to resist it. The researchers found that "the more frequently and recently participants had resisted any earlier desire, the less successful they were at resisting any other subsequent desire." In *Chocolat,* the mayor faced more and more challenges, each perhaps using a bit of the gas in his tank. And notice when he snapped: in the evening, after earlier having dealt with a major town issue. His gas tank was empty. Interestingly, Baumeister's team found that desires to use social media were "especially prone to be enacted despite resistance." Perhaps this comes as less of a surprise now that we have a better sense of how addictive our devices of distraction can be.

Is there hope for the majority of us who don't have a well-developed System 2? As Arnsten hinted, it can be helpful to keep our System 2 gas tank full. Simple things like making sure we get enough sleep, stay fed, and so forth can be helpful. Keeping our stress levels low may be another story.

Since we can't think our way to well-being, and getting caught up in planning or other types of daydreaming might increase our stress levels and the sense of disconnection in our lives, seeing how these processes work, ideally and in real life, can be a first step forward. Seeing what it is like when we aren't paying attention to our significant others or kids can help clarify the actual rewards that we get from our distractions. Pulling out our stress compass and paying attention to the pull of the beep or blip can help us step back, right in the moment, rather than becoming glued to our phones yet again.

5

Addicted to Thinking

One of the greatest addictions, you never read about it in the papers because the people who are addicted to it don't know it, is the addiction to thinking.

—*Eckhart Tolle*

When I was first learning to meditate, one of the practices was to use my breath as an object. The aim was to have this anchor to help keep my mind in the present moment without drifting off. The instruction was simple: pay attention to your breath, and when your mind wanders, bring it back. When the boat starts to drift, the anchor catches the ocean floor. I remember going to the Insight Meditation Society (IMS, a well-respected retreat center founded by Joseph Goldstein, Sharon Salzburg, and Jack Kornfield) to practice paying attention to my breath for nine days on a retreat. Nothing but silence and my breath. Even better, IMS's retreat center is located in Barre, Massachusetts, and since I was there in December, I didn't have the distraction of wanting to go for walks in their woods. It was too cold.

That retreat was rough. I would sweat through T-shirts during the meditation periods and take naps every chance I got. I felt like the mayor in *Chocolat*, wrestling with my personal devil. No matter what I tried, I just couldn't get my thoughts under control. When I look back at my highlight reel of the retreat, one scene always gives me a chuckle. I had an individual interview with the Vietnamese monk who was leading the retreat. Through a translator, I told him how I would try this or that technique to knock my thoughts out. I even told him how my body got really hot during meditation. He nodded and smiled and, through the translator, said, "Ah good, burning off the fetters!" My coach, who thought I was doing great, was giving me a pep talk before the bell rang for the next round of fighting.

I didn't know it at the time, but I was addicted to something in particular—thinking. For a long time, I had been getting seduced by or caught up in my own thoughts. Once I recognized that tendency, a great many things fell into place. The recruitment video for Princeton was entitled "Conversations That Matter." Yes, I wanted to attend a college where I could stay up until the wee hours of the morning, engrossed in deep conversation with my roommates. I did (behavior). It felt great (reward). Always up for the challenge, I remember going back and solving synthetic organic chemistry problems that I got wrong on the exam. While working in my thesis lab, I once did a series of synthetic steps to make a new organic molecule. After purifying the new compound to determine whether the experiment had gone according to plan, I kept going through my data and then back and forth with my advisor, offering different ideas about what it could be. At some point I had an "aha!" moment and finally figured it out. I rushed to show this to my advisor, who, with a hearty "good job," confirmed my conclusions. I was so proud that I had figured it out that for weeks afterward when there were dull moments in lab, I would pull out my data and stare at them to relive the experience.

Fast-forward to medical and graduate school, where emphasis was placed on quick and clear thinking. In medical school, we were frequently questioned, or "pimped,"[1] by our resident physician supervisors and professors about our knowledge, and praised (reward-ed) if we came up with the correct answers. As with my undergradu-ate thesis work, in graduate school we were rewarded for solving sci-entific problems and presenting the results on posters or in talks at conferences. The ultimate reward was to see our research pass peer review: publication. I spent way too much time getting sucked into my own subjectively biased worldview: cursing reviewers for not see-ing the brilliance of our work, and praising them when they did. And when I had a tough day in graduate school, just as I had done with my data as an undergrad, I would pull out my papers and stare at them to feel that jolt of excited warmth at seeing our research (and my name) in print.

Back to Barre, where I was sweating my butt off in the middle of winter on a meditation retreat. I thought I was supposed to stop thinking. I was trying to stop something that I had been rewarded for again and again. My mind was like a massive ship, cruising at speed. With all that inertia behind it, dropping an anchor wasn't going to work.

Thinking Is Not the Problem

At Princeton, my organic chemistry professor and future advisor (Maitland Jones Jr.), was well known for his excellent teaching. This was a good thing, because organic chemistry, or "orgo," was often viewed as a class to be endured rather than sought out, especially for premeds, students taking the class because it was a prerequisite for applying to medical school. To spice things up a bit, it was common throughout the year for students to play pranks on Professor Jones. The pranks were pretty benign, such as everyone pretending to read a newspaper at the start of class (imagine 200 students doing this in unison) a week after he had (rightly) admonished a student for reading the paper in class. More than happily, I had participated in the pranks and had even helped orchestrate some of them.

Toward the end of my second semester of orgo, Professor Jones called me into his office. Not that long before, another student and I had coated his beloved classroom blackboard with Pam cooking spray. When he walked into class that day and realized that he was going to have a heck of a time diagramming molecular synthetic pathways, he launched into a tirade about which types of pranks were and weren't acceptable. When he finished with "whoever did this should be expelled," it was pretty plain that our prank fell into the latter category. Directly after that class, my friend and I confessed and cleaned up the mess. It seemed that amends had been made. Why was I being called into his office?

As I entered his office, he called me over to his desk and motioned me to look at something in front of him. I didn't know what to expect. There I saw a computer printout that he was covering with another piece of paper. Ever so slowly, he slid the top piece of paper down so that I could read the top line. It was his class grade sheet. I was really confused. Why was he showing me this? Then he slid it down a little more: #1. Judson Brewer A+. "Congratulations," he said, beaming, "you got the top grade! You earned it." I liked orgo a lot, but was never expecting this! My nucleus accumbens must have lit up like a Christmas tree with the amount of dopamine that was surging through it at that moment. I was on a roller coaster: thrilled, excited, and speechless. Why can I write this in such vivid detail? Because that is what dopamine does: it helps us develop context-dependent memories—especially in moments of uncertainty. Boom—fireworks for the brain.

Most of us can recall those great moments in life. With amazing vividness and clarity, we remember the look in our spouse's eyes when he or she said, "I do." We remember everything about the hospital room where our first child was born. We also relive the *feel* of these experiences—the emotional thrills and chills that come with these events. And we can thank our brains for a job well done when we do.

Obviously, the fact that we are set up to remember events isn't a problem. That ability is a survival mechanism, whether it involves making it easier to remember the location of food (for our prehistoric ancestors) or helping us through a bad stretch during graduate school. Thinking is not the bad guy, either. Solving a math problem in school or coming up with a new deal at work helps us progress in life. Planning a vacation helps it happen—kind of hard to fly to Paris if we haven't bought the plane tickets.

Yet we can start to see how our little helper, dopamine, can get underfoot. When the subject is "me," we spend too much time posting pictures on Instagram or checking Facebook. When we are blinded by subjective bias, our simulations can't predict correctly and just take up time and mental energy. When we are restless or bored, we drop into a daydream about our wedding day or something exciting planned for the future.

In other words, thinking and all that goes with it (simulating, planning, remembering) is not the problem. It is only a problem when we get caught up in it.

Tripping on Thoughts

Lori "Lolo" Jones is an Olympic hurdler. Born in Iowa in 1982, she set the state high school record in the 100-meter hurdles, and she went on to become an eleven-time All-American at Louisiana State University. She won her first U.S. indoor championship in 2007, followed by an outdoor championship in 2008—and an Olympic berth. Not bad.

At the 2008 Olympics, in Beijing, Jones ran well, advancing to the finals of the 100-meter hurdles. And then what happened? Kevin Spain, a Louisiana reporter, wrote about that final race:

> By the third hurdle, Lolo Jones had caught her competition. By the fifth hurdle, she was in the lead. By the eighth hurdle, she was pulling away from the field in the Olympic final of the women's 100-meter hurdles.
>
> Two hurdles, nine strides and 64 feet separated the former LSU standout from a gold medal, and more important, fulfillment of a four-year quest and a lifelong dream.
>
> Then disaster struck.[2]

Jones clipped the ninth of ten hurdles, so instead of winning an Olympic gold, she finished seventh. In an interview with *Time* magazine four years later, she said, "I was just in an amazing rhythm . . . I knew at one point I was winning the race. It wasn't like, Oh, I'm winning the Olympic gold medal. It just seemed like another race. And then there was a point after that where . . . I was telling myself to make sure my legs were snapping out. So I overtried. I tightened up a bit too much. That's when I hit the hurdle."[3]

Jones's experience is a great example of the difference between thinking and *getting caught up* in thinking. She had plenty of thoughts go through her head during the race. It was only when she started to get in her own way, telling herself to make sure her technique was correct, that she "overtried." She literally tripped herself up.

In sports, music, and business, where success can come down to a single race, performance, or moment, it is really helpful to prepare, to be coached, and to practice over and over until we have it down. Then, when the big moment comes, our coaches tell us to just get out there and do it. Perhaps they even smile and say, "Have fun" so that we will relax. Why? Because we can't run our best race or nail a musical performance if we are tense. In overtrying, Jones "tightened up" and tripped.

This type of contraction may give us a few clues about what happens when we get caught up in our own thought patterns. Experientially, this entanglement can literally be felt as a clenching, grasping, or tightening feeling, both mentally and physically. Try this as a thought experiment: imagine what would happen if we spent fifteen minutes excitedly detailing a new idea to a coworker, and then he dismissed it out of hand with the comment "Well, that's a dumb idea!" Do we close down, walk away, and then ruminate on the encounter for the next several hours? Do we end up with stiffened shoulders at the end of the day because of the tension we carried around after the painful encounter? And what happens if we can't shake it off?

The late psychologist Susan Nolen-Hoeksema was very interested in what happens when people think "repetitively and passively about their negative emotions."[4] In other words, what happens when people get caught up in what she termed "ruminative response styles." For example, if we responded ruminatively to our colleague in the above example telling us that our idea was stupid, we might get caught up in worrying that it *was* a dumb idea, and that might lead to us think that *all* our ideas were dumb, when normally we might have shrugged off the comment (or agreed that the idea was dumb and dropped it).

Not surprisingly, several studies have shown that people who respond this way when feeling sad demonstrate higher levels of depressive symptoms over time.[5] Rumination—being caught up in repetitive thought loops—can even predict the chronicity, or persistence, of depression. To be fair, rumination has long been a topic of debate among clinicians and researchers. Several arguments have been put forth claiming that it confers some type of selective advantage, yet none has been satisfactory enough to bring the field into agreement. Might viewing it from an evolutionary vantage point of reward-based learning help fill in some gaps? Could rumination be another example of being "addicted" (continued use despite adverse consequence) to a certain way of thinking?

In a recent study entitled "Sad as a Matter of Choice? Emotion-Regulation Goals in Depression," Yael Millgram and colleagues showed depressed and nondepressed people happy, sad, or neutral pictures, then gave them a choice to see the same image again or a black screen, and finally asked them to rate their mood.[6] Across both groups, looking at happy pictures evoked happiness, while sad images evoked sadness. Pretty straightforward. Now here is where it got interesting. Compared with the nondepressed, depressed people did not differ in how many times they chose to look at happy pictures, yet they chose to view significantly more sadness-inducing images. As good scientists, Millgram and his team repeated their experiment with a new set of participants in the same setup, but instead of showing happy and sadness-inducing pictures, they had them listen to happy and sad music clips. They found the same effect: depressed people were more likely to choose sad music.

They then took it one step farther. They wondered what would happen if depressed people were given a cognitive strategy to make themselves feel either better or worse. Which would they choose? A final round of participants was trained in how to either increase or decrease their reactions to emotional stimuli. They were then shown the same types of happy, sad, and neutral images as in the first experiment and were asked to choose a strategy—make me happier or make me sadder. We can guess how this story ends. Indeed, depressed people chose not to make themselves feel better, but worse. This might sound strange to anyone who is not depressed. But to those with depression, it might sound or even feel familiar. They may simply be more accustomed to feeling this way. This is a sweater that fits, perhaps one that has become molded to their body because they have worn it so much. As part of this, rumination may be a mode of thinking that depressed people have reinforced to the point that it, in some way, authenticates *who they are*. Yes, this is me: I am that depressed guy. As Millgram and colleagues put it, "They may be motivated to experience sadness to verify their emotional selves."

Our Default Mode

We now have some clues that may link the types of thinking in which we can get caught up with how our brains work. Let's start with daydreaming. Malia Mason and colleagues set out to study what happens in the brain during mind wandering.[7] They trained volunteers to proficiency in some tasks, specifically, ones so boring "that their minds could wander," and compared brain activity during these tasks and novel tasks. They found that during the practiced tasks, the medial prefrontal cortex and the posterior cingulate cortex become relatively more activated that they did during performance of the novel ones. Recall that these are the midline brain structures involved in Kahneman's System 1, which seems to be involved in self-reference—becoming activated when something relevant to us is happening, such as thinking about ourselves or craving a cigarette. In fact, Mason's group found a direct correlation between the frequency of mind wandering and brain activity in these two regions. Around the same time, a research group led by Daniel Weissman likewise found that lapses in attention were linked to increased activity in these brain regions.[8] Our attention lapses, we fall into a daydream, or we start thinking about something we need to do later in the day, and then these brain regions light up.

The medial prefrontal cortex and the posterior cingulate cortex form the backbone of a network called the default mode network (DMN). The exact functions of the DMN are still debated, yet because of its prominence in self-referential processing, we can think of it functioning as the "me" network—linking ourselves to our inner and outer worlds. For example, recalling a memory about myself in a particular situation, choosing which of two cars to buy, or deciding whether an adjective describes me all activate the DMN, likely because these thoughts share the common feature of me: *I'm remembering, I'm deciding.*

This might sound a bit confusing, so some explanation of this network's discovery may help. The DMN was serendipitously discovered by Marc Raichle and colleagues at Washington University in St. Louis around 2000. The serendipity comes in because he had been using a task that his research group called "resting state" as a baseline comparison task for his experiments. In fMRI research, relative changes in blood flow during two tasks are compared. We measure brain activity during state A and subtract the activity recorded during state B (the baseline) to get a relative measure. This process helps control for baseline differences in someone's brain activity from day to day, and in activity from person to person. Raichle's group used something so simple that anyone could do it without practice. The instruction was (and continues to be): "Lay still and don't do anything in particular"—this was the resting state, the baseline.

The mystery came when the scientists started looking at "network connectivity," that is, the extent to which brain regions were activated or deactivated at the same time. It is assumed that if there is a tight synchrony in the timing of different regions' firing, they are likely to be "functionally coupled," as if they were communicating with one another more than with any of the other brain regions they were coupled with. Raichle's group repeatedly found that the medial prefrontal cortex and posterior cingulate cortex (and other regions) seemed to be talking to each other during the resting-state task. But we aren't supposed to be doing anything during rest, right? This was the big question. Raichle, a very careful scientist, repeated his experiments and analyses over and over. He sat on his data for several years and finally published his first report, entitled, "Medial Prefrontal Cortex and Self-Referential Mental Activity: Relation to a Default Mode of Brain Function," in 2001.[9]

Over the next few years, more and more published reports like those of Mason and Weissman showed correlations and suggested links between the DMN, self-referential processing, and mind wandering. Killingsworth's study showing that we mind-wander half the day fit nicely here—perhaps the DMN was aptly named if we default to daydreaming. A decade after Raichle's seminal paper was published, Sue Whitfield-Gabrieli, a neuroscientist at MIT, put the last nail in the coffin of uncertainty.[10] She designed an elegantly simple experiment: she had people perform an explicitly self-referential task (looking at adjectives and deciding whether the words described them) and the resting-state task (don't do anything in particular). Instead of using the resting state as a baseline, she directly compared the two and found that indeed they both activated the medial prefrontal and posterior cingulate cortices. This research might sound like tedious and boring work, yet direct comparison and replication studies in neuroscience are hard to come by. Remember novelty and dopamine? Maybe scientists and editors reviewing papers submitted for publication aren't as excited by confirmation studies as by those announcing the discovery of something new.

While Whitfield-Gabrieli was linking self-referential thinking to DMN activity, my lab was investigating what happens in the brains of expert meditators. I had seen some remarkable results in my clinical studies, and we wanted to see whether and how meditation affected brain activity. We started by comparing brain activity in novice and expert meditators. The experts came in with an average of more than ten thousand hours of practice, whereas we taught the novices three types of meditation on the morning of their fMRI scan.

We taught the novices three common, well-known types of formal meditation:

1. Awareness of the breath: Pay attention to your breath, and when your mind wanders, bring it back.
2. Loving-kindness: Think of a time when you genuinely wished someone well. Using this feeling as a focus, silently wish all beings well by repeating a few short phrases of your choosing over and over. For example: May all beings be happy, may all beings be healthy, may all beings be safe from harm.
3. Choiceless awareness: Pay attention to whatever comes into your awareness, whether it is a thought, emotion, or bodily sensation. Just follow it until something else comes into your awareness, not trying to hold onto it or change it in any way. When something else comes into your awareness, just pay attention to it until the next thing comes along.

Why these three meditations? We wanted to see what they had in common. Our hope was that the results would give us a handle on or a doorway into brain patterns that might be universal and shared across different contemplative and religious communities.

We analyzed our data, excitedly anticipating that we would find some type of increased activation in our expert meditators. They were *doing* something after all in meditating. Meditating is not resting—far from it, or so we thought. Yet when we looked across the entire brain, we couldn't find a single region that showed more activity in experts than in novices. We scratched our heads. We looked again. We still didn't find anything.

We then looked to see whether any brain regions showed *decreased* activity in experts relative to novices. Bingo! We found four, two of which were the medial prefrontal cortex and the posterior

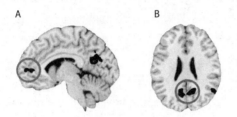

A   B

Default mode network deactivation during meditation. *A,* During meditation, expert meditators show less activity in the medial prefrontal cortex (shown in the circled region, as viewed from the side of the head) and the posterior cingulate cortex (PCC). *B,* Alternate view of the PCC (shown in the circled region, as viewed from above the head). Reproduced with permission from J. A. Brewer et al., "Meditation Experience Is Associated with Differences in Default Mode Network Activity and Connectivity," *Proceedings of the National Academy of Sciences* 108, no. 50 (2011): 20254–59.

cingulate cortex, the central hubs of the DMN. Many peripheral brain regions connect to them.[11] They are like hub cities that link flights from across the country for major airlines. The involvement of these brain areas in our results couldn't be a coincidence.

Convergence in the Center (of the Brain)

Following the lead of Raichle, I wanted to be cautious about our findings. More importantly, I wanted to repeat our experiments to make sure what we had found wasn't a statistical fluke or simply a re-sult of the small number of meditators (twelve in each group). We set out to recruit additional experienced meditators, and at the same time I started talking to a colleague, Xenios Papademetris, about doing more than just a replication study.

After receiving his PhD in electrical engineering from Yale in 2000, Xenios spent a decade developing novel methods to improve medical imaging. When I met him, he had developed an entire bioimaging suite that was freely available for researchers processing and analyzing electroencephalography (EEG) and fMRI data. Xenios was now work-ing with a tall, unassuming graduate student named Dustin Scheinost to speed up the process so that researchers and subjects could see fMRI results in real time. They were in effect making one the world's most expensive neurofeedback devices, which would allow someone to see and get feedback on his or her own brain activity instantly. The price tag was worth it. Neurofeedback from fMRI scans provided a level of spatial accuracy that was unprecedented: devices such as an EEG only went skin deep, literally, whereas Xenios's setup could give localized feedback from a region *the size of a peanut* anywhere in the brain.

I tested Xenios and Dustin's real-time fMRI neurofeedback by meditating in the fMRI scanner while watching a graph of my posterior cingulate cortex (PCC) activity. Basically, I lay on my back in our MRI machine, meditating with my eyes open while I watched a graph plot changes in my brain activity every couple of seconds. I would meditate on an object—for example, my breath—and after a short period of time, I would check the graph to see how it lined up with my experience, then return to meditation. Since brain activity is measured relative to a baseline condition, we set up a procedure in which I would see adjectives flash on a screen in the scanner for thirty seconds, much as Whitfield-Gabrieli had done for her task. After thirty seconds, the graph would start to appear, showing whether my

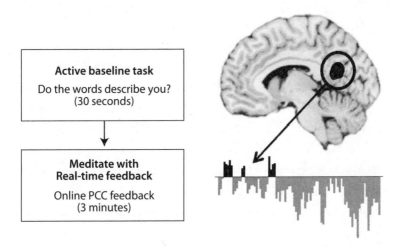

Schematic of neurofeedback protocol. An active baseline task is followed by meditation with real-time feedback. During meditation, the percent signal change in the PCC (corrected for global brain activity) is calculated and plotted in real time. Reproduced with permission from J. A. Brewer and K. A. Garrison, "The Posterior Cingulate Cortex as a Plausible Mechanistic Target of Meditation: Findings from Neuroimaging," *Annals of the New York Academy of Sciences* 1307, no. 1 (2014): 19–27.

PCC activity was increasing or decreasing. A new bar would fill in next to the previous one every two seconds as the scanner measured my brain activity and updated the results. Although fMRI measurement of brain activity leads to a slight delay in the signal, the procedure worked surprisingly well. I could link my subjective experience of meditation with my brain activity virtually in real time.

After numerous rounds of pilot testing our new contraption, we set up our second meditation study much like the first: participants were asked to pay attention to their breath as their primary object of meditation. But this time we had them meditate while receiving real-time fMRI neurofeedback: eyes open, being mindful of their breathing, and then checking in with the graph from time to time to see how well their brain activity lined up with awareness of their breath. In this way, we could more closely link the participants' subjective experiences with their brain activity. Previously, we had to wait to ask people after each run, on average, about their experience of meditation, such as how focused or distracted they were when paying attention to their breath. And we had no way of analyzing their data in real time, let alone showing them their brain activity from that run. Over a five-minute period, a lot happens moment to moment. All those moments got mashed together as we calculated an average brain signal—often months after the last subject's data were collected. We wanted to see whether we could home in with much greater precision on what was happening in any particular moment. How active was the brain at a given instant? We were moving into a field of study called neurophenomenology—exploring the conjunction between our momentary subjective experience and our brain activity. And we were in unchartered territory in the field of cognitive neuroscience.

The next two years were some of the most interesting and exciting of my career. We learned something from almost every person, whether novice or experienced meditator, who signed up for our neurofeedback study. By focusing on giving feedback from the PCC (we were set up to give feedback from only one region at a time), we could see, virtually in real time, substantive differences between the brain activity of novice and experienced meditators. For example, we would see a lot of variability in PCC activity during a run with a novice, who immediately afterward would report, "Yep, my mind was all over the place, as you can see there and there and there [referring to specific points on the graph]."

Experienced meditators, not being familiar with seeing their own brain activity during their usual practice, first had to learn how to meditate while viewing the graph—it isn't every day that we get to watch our mental activity while meditating. For example, we would see the graph go up at the beginning as they adjusted to having a potentially very distracting and seductive graph of their own brain

Experienced meditator learning to watch his brain activity in real time while meditating. The black bars above the horizontal line indicate increases in PCC activity, and grey bars below the horizontal line indicate decreases in PCC activity during meditation, relative to the active baseline (deciding whether certain adjectives described someone). Each bar indicates a two-second measurement. Laboratory archives of Judson Brewer.

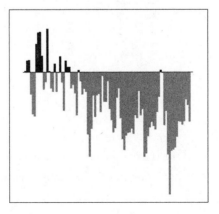

activity appear, and then drop down and down as they got deeper into meditation and weren't pulled to look at the graph. Imagine what this was like for them: something right in front of their face was showing them how their brain was reacting during a practice some of them had been doing every day for decades, yet they had to stay focused on their breath.

Other runs by experienced meditators would show a long period of decreased PCC activity and then a big spike followed by another drop. They would report that their meditation had been going well, but when they checked in with the graph or had a thought like "Look how well I'm doing!" the disruption would register as a big increase in brain activity.

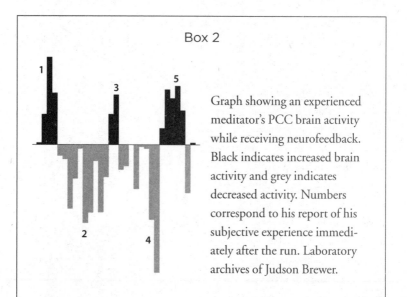

Box 2

Graph showing an experienced meditator's PCC brain activity while receiving neurofeedback. Black indicates increased brain activity and grey indicates decreased activity. Numbers correspond to his report of his subjective experience immediately after the run. Laboratory archives of Judson Brewer.

Here is an example of an experienced meditator who did a short, one-minute meditation while watching his brain activity (posterior cingulate cortex). Immediately after the run was over, he reported on how his subjective experience lined up with the graph.

1. So at the beginning, I caught myself, that I was sort of trying to guess when the words were going to end [baseline task] and when the meditation was going to begin. So I was kind of trying to be like, "Okay, ready, set, go!" and then there was an additional word that popped up, and I was like, "Oh shit," and so that's the [black] spike you see there . . .
2. . . . and then I sort of immediately settled in, and I was really getting into it . . . (first run of grey)
3. . . . and then I thought, "Oh my gosh, this is amazing" (second black spike)
4. . . . and I was like, "Okay, wait, don't get distracted," and then I got back into it, and then it got [grey] again . . . (second run of grey)
5. "Oh my gosh, this is unbelievable, it's doing exactly what my mind is doing," and so then it got [black] again . . . (last bit of black)

We found novices whose brain activity looked more like that of experts. Like people who have a gift for being present and not getting caught up in their own stories, they could steadily decrease PCC activity. By the same token, we found experienced meditators whose brain patterns were more in line with what we saw with novices: their moment-to-moment brain activity was all over the place. And most interestingly, both novice and experienced meditators reported learning something about their experience, even though the experiment was *not* set up as a learning paradigm. It was intended only to confirm our previous results showing that decreased PCC activity correlated with meditation.

For example, the brains of several novices showed a great deal of increased PCC activity in the first three runs (each lasting three minutes, so nine minutes total). Then suddenly, on the next run, their brains would show a huge drop in activity. One novice reported that he "focused more on the physical sensation instead of thinking 'in' and 'out' [of breathing]." Another reported that the drop correlated with feeling "a lot more relaxed, like it was less of a struggle to prevent my mind from wandering."

These folks were using their brain feedback as a way to correct their meditation. Similar to Lolo Jones tripping herself up by overtrying and tightening up, our participants were seeing in real time what it is like to get caught up *trying* to meditate. Previously, we hadn't factored in the trying bit—the quality or attitude of their awareness, so to speak—into our models. These results made us take a fresh look at how we were conceptualizing meditation.

We did all sorts of control experiments to make sure our participants weren't fooling themselves. It can be pretty easy to trust what a big fancy machine is telling us rather than our own experience. We also made sure that experienced meditators could manipulate their PCC activity *on demand*—and that they could flex this "mental muscle" when prompted.

After collecting this extraordinary neurophenomenological data, we handed them all over to a colleague at Brown, Cathy Kerr, and an undergraduate who was working with her, Juan Santoyo. Juan had not been privy to our testing methods or goals, so he knew nothing of our hypothesis that decreased PCC activity correlated with meditation. He was thus the perfect person to make verbatim transcriptions of the subjective reports, mark at what time they happened during the run, and categorize them into bins of experience such as "concentration," "observing sensory experience," "distraction," and so on. After binning the participants' subjective experiences, Juan could use the time stamps to line up their experience with their brain activity.

Results

The results of this experiment showed two things. First, they confirmed what previous studies had found regarding PCC activity, averaged across a number of participants: it decreased when people concentrated (in this case during meditation) and increased when people were distracted or their minds wandered, as Mason's and Weissman's work showed. This "positive control" nicely linked our paradigm with previous studies. Yet it didn't seem to tell us anything unique about meditation and PCC activity.

Here is where the second, surprising result came in. One of the bins that Juan filled was called "controlling"—trying to control one's experience. That activity lined up with increases in PCC activity. Another, labeled "effortless doing," correlated with decreased PCC activity. Taken together, these data revealed the mode of subjective experience that lined up with PCC activity—not perception of an object, but *how we relate to it*. In a sense, if we try to control a situation (or our lives), we have to work hard at *doing* something to get the results we want. In contrast, we can relax into an attitude that is more like a dance with the object, simply *being* with it as the situation unfolds, no striving or struggling necessary, as we get out of our own way and rest in an awareness of what is happening moment to moment.

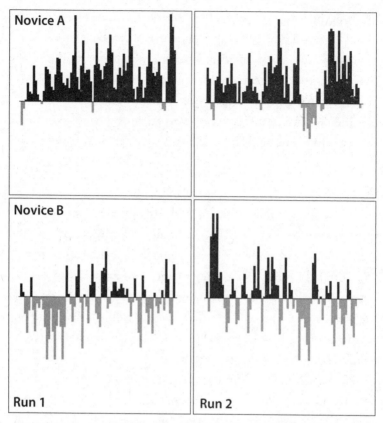

Novice A

Novice B

Run 1   **Run 2**

Novice meditators show decreased PCC activity as they learn the nuances of meditation through real-time fMRI neurofeedback. PCC activity was shown to participants for three-minute blocks while they meditated with their eyes open. Increases in PCC activity relative to baseline are shown in black; decreases are shown in grey. Participants reported on their

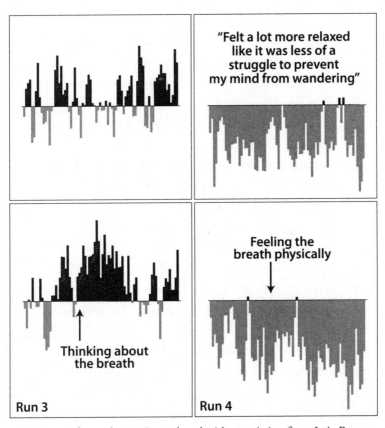

experiences after each run. Reproduced with permission from J. A. Brewer and K. A. Garrison, "The Posterior Cingulate Cortex as a Plausible Mechanistic Target of Meditation: Findings from Neuroimaging," *Annals of the New York Academy of Sciences* 1307, no. 1 (2014): 19–27.

After our findings started to come together, I called Dr. Whitfield-Gabrieli to get a second opinion on our data. We agreed that it made sense that experienced meditators would not get caught up in mind wandering as much as novices did. Had this aspect of experience been reported previously? We agreed to work together to look at all the published papers that we could find related to PCC activation. Together with a postdoctoral fellow of mine, Katie Garrison, we combed through the literature, collecting a number of studies that reported on changes in PCC activity, regardless of task or paradigm.

We ended up with a long and seemingly hodgepodge list that included Raichle's resting state, Mason's mind wandering, and other papers related to self-reference. But we also saw studies showing increased PCC activity with, among other things, choice justification (liking a choice you made), obsessive-compulsive disorder, emotional processing (including ruminative thinking in depressed individuals), guilt, induced immoral behavior, and craving. Remember the study by Sherman and colleagues (discussed in chapter 2) that measured adolescents' brain activity while viewing an Instagram feed? The more likes one of their pictures received, the greater the PCC activity.

What could explain such a variety of studies? After some thought and some back-and-forth, we decided to apply Occam's razor. This philosophical or scientific rule states that quantities should not be multiplied needlessly. In science, it implies that the simplest explanation should be given priority over more complex ones, and that the explanation for an unknown phenomenon should first be looked for in known quantities or events. In that spirit, we wondered whether there was some concept underlying all our data as well as the previously published research. Taking what we had learned from our neurophenomenological data set and applying it to the other studies, the most parsimonious explanation came down to the same reason why Lolo tripped. Our data were directly pointing to something experiential.

These brain studies of the default mode network may reveal something important in our everyday lives that we can start to pay more attention to—namely, getting caught up in the push and pull of our experience. On my meditation retreat, I really bore down, fighting my addictive thinking and trying to push it away. If we become habituated or even addicted to a certain way of thinking, whether simple daydreaming or a more complex ruminative response style, it can be hard to keep from getting caught up in "stinkin' thinkin,'" as my patients with alcohol use disorders like to say. Our brain data filled in a critical piece of the puzzle: how our thoughts, feelings, and behaviors relate *to us*. A thought is simply a word or an image in our mind until we think it is so great and so exciting that we can't get it out of our heads. A craving is just a craving unless we get sucked into it.

How we *relate* to our thoughts and feelings makes all the difference.

Meditators train themselves to notice these experiences and not get caught up in them—to simply see them for what they are and *not take them personally*. The PCC may be linking us to our experiences through reward-based learning. Through mental and physical contraction, we may be learning that "we" are thinking, "we" are craving. And through this connection, we form a strong relationship to our thoughts and feelings. We learn to see the world through a particular set of glasses over and over, to the point that we take the view they provide at face value as who we are. The self itself isn't a problem, since remembering who we are when we wake up each morning is very helpful. Instead, the problem is the extent to which we get caught up in the drama of our lives and take it personally when something happens to us (good or bad). Whether we get lost in a daydream, a ruminative thought pattern, or a craving, we feel a bit of tightening, narrowing, shrinking, or closing down in our bodies and minds. Whether it is excitement or fear, that hook always gets us.

6

Addicted to Love

Love is strong as death,
passion fierce as the grave.
Its flashes are flashes of fire,
A raging flame.

—*Song of Solomon* 8:6 *(New Revised Standard Version)*

In a moment of lightheartedness that science rarely sees, researchers at Stanford University sponsored "The Love Competition." Using an fMRI machine, they scanned people's brains while they were mentally "loving on" their special someone. The competition was to see who could activate the brain's reward centers the most. The scanning focused on the nucleus accumbens. Contestants had five minutes "to love someone as hard as they can." Why would the researchers zero in on a reward center of the brain linked to addiction?

My Chemical Romance

The summer after college graduation, my girlfriend (and newly minted fiancée) and I went on a weeklong backpacking trip in Colorado. On the drive back to the East Coast, we stopped in St. Louis, where we were both about to start medical school, and the rest of our lives, together. Within an hour of signing leases for apartments a few doors down from each other, we broke up.

"Mary" and I had started dating during our sophomore year at Princeton. We had what I would guess to be a storybook college romance. Both being serious musicians, we played in the orchestra together (she the flute, and I the violin). She studied chemical engineering, I chemistry. We studied together. We ate together. We socialized together. We argued at times, but quickly made up. We were passionately in love.

During our senior year, we both applied to the same large list of MD-PhD programs. The Medical Scientist Training Program, as it was officially titled, afforded an opportunity for people interested in both taking care of patients and doing medical research to earn both degrees at an intense, accelerated pace. The kicker was that it was free—anyone who was accepted had their tuition paid by federal grant money, and even received a small stipend for living expenses. Which meant there weren't many slots and the competition was fierce. That fall was pretty nerve-racking as Mary and I waited to hear whether either or both of us would be invited to interview—and at the same institution. Along with my roommates, one of whom was also applying to MD-PhD programs and another who was applying for jobs, I would tape rejection letters to the wall of our dorm room. We would then take turns adding a handwritten PS to one another's letters as a form of stress relief: "PS. YOU SUCK!" "GO USA" (the 1996 Olympics were in Atlanta the next summer), and any other variation of off-the-wall or random insult we could think of.

Mary and I were ecstatic when, in December, we both were accepted to Washington University in St. Louis. It was one of our top choices, given its reputation for excellence and its student support. The program administrator leaked to us that the admissions committee was very happy to accept this "lovely young couple" and looked forward to us joining the university's ranks. We started envisioning spending the rest of our lives together, supporting each other as we both learned medicine. We would come home to each other after a long day in the lab and help each other solve scientific problems over a glass of wine. It was perfect.

Over the holiday break that winter, I was on cloud nine. My brain kept simulating our future together. All the predictions showed success and happiness. So I decided to take the obvious next step: to ask her to marry me. I bought a ring, brought it back to campus, and planned the proposal. To match my outlook, I planned big.

I mapped out all the meaningful people, places, and things from our previous two years together and set up a treasure hunt of sorts where she would have to follow clues from one spot on campus to another. When she arrived at each new location, she would be greeted by one of our good friends or prized professors who would hand her a red rose and an envelope. Each envelope contained a few puzzle pieces; at the end of the hunt, all the pieces could be assembled to spell out, "Will you e-mail me?" It sounds dorky (and it was), but e-mail was just coming into use at the time, so I was excited to use it as the final clue. In her e-mail, she would read a note sent from my best high school friend, telling her to go to the top floor of the math building, the tallest building on campus. The top floor offered a beautiful 360-degree view of the area. I had been bequeathed a rogue key to that floor by a student who had graduated; the area was mainly for entertaining, and off limits to unaccompanied students. Mary and I had sneaked up there before, and I thought it would be a great place to propose. My roommate would then come in, act as a waiter, and serve us dinner from our favorite restaurant.

The plan went off without a hitch on a beautiful, chilly, yet clear winter's day. All our friends and professors played their parts perfectly—they were as into it as I was. When we made it to the top of the tower, she said yes, and we finished the evening watching the sun set over the town of Princeton. Six months later, on a warm summer evening in St. Louis, we ended it.

Why am I oversharing? Remember how I told my smoking cessation groups at Yale that I "had plenty of addictions" (including thinking, as we explored in the last chapter)? Well, at that time I couldn't see straight. I might as well face it: I was addicted to love.

Think back to the last time you began a romantic relationship. What did those butterflies in your stomach feel like when you leaned in for that first kiss? Good enough to go in for a second one? As the romance heated up, you were full of energy; life seemed wonderful. You would go on and on about how amazing your special person was to anyone who would listen. You couldn't get that person out of your head. And you couldn't wait for that next text, phone call, or date. Your friends may have even said that you were addicted to this person. As with the high of other addictions, there is a flip side to this adulation, too: the irritability that comes when your special someone doesn't call you when he or she promised to, or the funk that you go into when that person is away for several days.

If we look at my college romance from a reward-based-learning perspective, the pieces of *that* puzzle start to fit. Yet again, I had unknowingly been seducing myself, reinforcing my subjective bias that she was *the one*. I downplayed our major religious differences. Mary was devoutly Catholic; I saw this as a chance to learn something new (ironically, I am now happily married to a devout Catholic). We never discussed kids; we would figure it out. We had blowout arguments in major public places (I sit here cringing as I think back to some of those). But who doesn't argue? When I asked her father if I could marry her, he said he thought we were too young (but said go ahead). I overheard Professor Jones saying the same thing to a colleague—what did they know about our relationship? One of my best friends, a graduate student who had already been divorced, pleaded with me not to do this—he could see that we were headed for trouble. I got angry and ignored him for weeks.

I was feeling so stoked and, yes, invincible that I ignored all the instruments on my cockpit dashboard. This plane wasn't running out of gas; it wasn't going to crash. I was fueling it on romance. Really, I was smoking the crack pipe of love. And though it took me six months to sober up and face the music, my final binge was our engagement day. Just look at how I set it up: one hit of excitement and anticipation after another.

There is nothing wrong with romantic love. In modern times, just like thinking and planning, it helps humans survive. It is when we get completely caught up in it, when things get out of control, that we crash and burn. It is perhaps another example of not knowing how to read our stress compass—dopamine leading us into danger instead of away from it.

Winning the Game of Love

Neuroscientists and psychologists have been trying to unpack the components of romantic love for decades. Early stages of it have been associated with euphoria, intense focus on and obsessive thinking about the romantic partner, emotional dependency, and even "craving for emotional union with this beloved."[1] Descriptions of romantic love dating back thousands of years regularly include reward-related images. For example, the speaker in the biblical Song of Songs exclaims, "How much better is your love than wine" (4:10). In her TED

Talk, the biological anthropologist Helen Fisher read a poem told by an anonymous Kwakiutl Indian of southern Alaska to a missionary in 1896: "Fire runs through my body with the pain of loving you. Pain runs through my body with the fires of my love for you. Pain like a boil about to burst with my love for you, consumed by fire with my love for you. I remember what you said to me. I am thinking of your love for me. I am torn by your love for me. Pain and more pain—where are you going with my love?"[2]

Noting that all this sounds a lot like addiction, Fisher teamed up with a psychologist, Arthur Aron, and other researchers to specifically test whether romantic love activated the same brain regions as drugs like alcohol, cocaine, and heroin, including what is called the ventral tegmental area, the source of dopamine in the reward circuit. They started by interviewing participants about the duration, intensity, and range of romantic love. Participants then completed the Passionate Love Scale, which used statements such as "For me, X is the perfect romantic partner" and "Sometimes I can't control my thoughts; they are obsessively on X." The scale is thought to be a reliable means of quantifying this complex sentiment.

Once subjects were determined to really be in love, the researchers put them in an fMRI scanner and had them view pictures of their romantic partner (the "active" condition) as well as a friend of the same sex (the "comparison" condition) while their brain activity was being measured. Remember: because there is no absolute measure for brain activity (that is, no "thermometer" on which we can line everyone up based on certain values), fMRI is used to measure increases or decreases in activity relative to something else—hence, the comparison condition (the baseline). Because it is difficult to quell intense feelings of romantic love, the researchers tried to distract the participants when they weren't viewing pictures of their love interests by having them do a boring math task, which would allow their brain activity to return to more normal or baseline levels. Think of this distraction as taking a mental cold shower.

Perhaps not surprisingly, the research team found increased activation in the dopamine-producing part of the brain (the ventral tegmental area) in response to feelings of romantic love. The more attractive the subjects had rated their partner, the more activated the area was. This result supported predictions that romantic love activates our brain's reward circuitry, as the endless stream of expressions of love—poems, art, songs—sent throughout the world would seem to suggest. As Fisher quipped, "Romantic love is one of the most addictive substances on Earth."

So who won Stanford's love competition? A seventy-five-year-old gentleman named Kent, who reported that he had met his wife on a blind date. Three days after their first encounter, the two were engaged to be married. In a short film documenting the competition, Kent said, "We were so madly in love. There were just bells and whistles immediately when we first met." He continued, "I can still feel the feeling," even though "that original intensity has moderated." The way he hugs his wife of fifty years at the end of the movie makes the truth of his statement beautifully clear.

As Kent hinted at, there could be something to the idea of still being able to *feel* those feelings of romance without getting caught up in them. Let's return to the study by Aron, Fisher, and colleagues mentioned earlier. The team looked at activity in the posterior cingulate cortex as well as in the brain's reward centers. The PCC, recall, is the brain region linked most consistently to self-reference. The previous chapter discussed how relative increases in PCC activity may be an indicator of "me"—taking things personally, getting caught up in them. What Aron's research team found was that the *shorter* one's romantic relationship, the *greater* the PCC activity. In other words, while someone's romance was still relatively novel or new, her PCC was likely to heat up. If someone was more settled in a relationship (as measured crudely by time), her PCC was quieter. Might this provide a clue about how we get caught up in the newness of a relationship or the thrill of the chase when things are fresh and we don't know how they will turn out? When we start dating someone new, we might do all sorts of nice things to woo the object of our affection. Yet who is it *really* about? Me.

In a follow-up study a few years later, Aron, Fisher, and colleagues used the same procedures as those in their earlier study, but sought out people in long-term relationships. These people had been happily married for more than ten years and still reported being very much in love. Here is the kicker. The researchers also measured a subscale of the Passionate Love Scale to see how brain activity lined up with a certain aspect of romance: obsession. Did people who were happily attached have the same brain activity patterns as obsessed teenagers, or were they more like mothers, who, in research by other groups, had shown reward circuit activation yet *decreases* in PCC activity?[3]

What did the researchers find? Averaging twenty-one years of monogamous yet still reportedly romantic marriage, volunteers for their study activated dopamine-based reward circuitry (ventral tegmental area) when thinking passionately about their spouses. Participants showed increased activation in the PCC overall, too, yet this activity could be differentiated by their obsession scores on the Passionate Love Scale: the more someone was obsessed with his partner, the greater the PCC activity. As Fisher put it in her TED talk describing love as an addiction, "You focus on the person, you obsessively think about them, you crave them, you distort reality." You. You. You. As in, me. Me. Me. Me. To some degree or another, we all can relate to this.

Early in a relationship, we look to see whether our potential partner is going to be a good fit for us. Later on, if one or both partners in a relationship retain this self-centeredness, things might not go as smoothly. If we plant the flag of "me" in the ground, declaring that we must have this or that, our relationship may go south. After all, addiction isn't about caring for one's children or saving the world. It is about getting sucked into the vortex of gratifying our desires, over and over and over. Does this difference between an obsessed love and the more "mature" type of love that Kent seemed to be showing suggest that there might be brain signatures for other types of love as well?

Love Is All You Need

The ancient Greeks had at least four words for love: *eros,* intimate or passionate love; *storge,* the affection between parents and children; *philia,* friendship; and *agape,* selfless love that is extended to all people.

The first three types of love are pretty straightforward. Agape can be more mysterious. For example, agape is used by Christians to express the unconditional love of God for God's children. The feeling can be reciprocal as well: the love of God for humans and of humans for God. In an attempt to capture the unconditional or selfless nature of the word, Latin writers translated *agape* as *caritas,* which is the origin of the English word "charity."

What exactly do these different concepts of love mean? As a scientist, I have had a hard time wrapping my mind around them. By the end of college, I certainly had a feel for the good, the bad, and the ugly of romantic love. What was this business about selfless love?

Not surprisingly, there is no storybook ending when romantic love falls apart. My parting from Mary was no different. As a result, at the beginning of medical school, and for the first time in my life, I had trouble sleeping. Compounding the trouble was the fact that Mary and I lived just a few doors from each other and were in the same classroom all day. I had picked up Jon Kabat-Zinn's *Full Catastrophe Living* a few weeks before classes began, since my life seemed to be fully catastrophic. I started listening to the meditation instructions on the first day of school, and thus began a new chapter of my life.

Every morning I would get up early, start listening to a cassette tape of a guided breath-awareness exercise, and at some point fall asleep. I did this diligently for about six months, until I could stay awake for half an hour. Then I started meditating during boring medical school lectures (why not?). After a year or two, I could start to see how meditation was helping me not get caught up in the many story lines simultaneously coursing through my head at any one moment (remember being addicted to thinking?). "Okay, this stuff might be helpful," I thought. I found a local meditation group. I started sitting with the group once a week. I listened to the teacher's talks and started reading more and more about meditation.

The teachings made sense, and I felt very much at home in them, especially as my practice deepened. Unlike the faith-based traditions that I had tried out, meditation was very much rooted in experience—which, I should point out, was a distinction indicating my naiveté and lack of experience with the divine (or even simply the words describing that experience) rather than a shortcoming of religion in general. "Don't believe what I say, try it for yourself," the Buddha is reported to have said. For example, when anxious, I could step back and check in with what I was thinking, and I would find that some exaggerated thought, usually about something in the future, was likely to be driving it.

One evening after our usual half-hour sitting meditation, the group leader started talking about loving-kindness, or *metta*, and that genuinely wishing people well, starting with ourselves, moving on to others, and eventually finishing with all beings, was the practice—and this type of thing had been done for thousands of years. I balked. I didn't care how long this or that might have been traditionally done, how did loving-kindness have anything to do with me being caught up in my own story line, let alone *me* causing *my own* suffering? I bargained with myself that I could use this as a concentration practice, as the teaching stated, period. Say the phrases. Notice whether the mind wanders to something else. Return to the phrases. No hokey touchy-feely stuff.

It was only after several more years of practicing loving-kindness that it began to dawn on me what selfless love actually *felt* like. By the time I began residency training, I was starting to notice a warmth in my chest, a loosening up of some type of contraction in my body when I was doing the practice. Not all the time, but sometimes. I was certainly intimately familiar with the excited, contracted type of romantic love. Might this different feeling be *metta?*

While in residency, I started playing with this idea, performing different personal experiments. For example, when riding my bike to work, I definitely felt a contraction when someone honked or yelled at me. I noticed that I had been getting into a weird reward dynamic: get honked at (trigger); yell, gesture, or purposefully ride in front of the car (behavior); feel self-righteous (reward). I would bring that contracted self-righteousness into the hospital as I complained about my run-ins to other physicians.

Noticing that I wasn't exactly bringing good cheer to my patients, I started testing what would happen to my contraction (and attitude) if, instead of yelling at the cars, I used their honks as a trigger to practice loving-kindness. First, a phrase to myself, "May I be happy," and then a phrase to the driver, "May you be happy." This helped break the cycle of self-righteousness and the contracted feeling that went along with it. Great—this was helping. After a little while longer, I noticed that I was arriving at work in a much lighter state. The contractedness was gone. Then it hit me: I don't have to wait until someone honks at me to practice wishing people well. I can do it with anyone I see. I started arriving at work positively joyful on most days. This stuff seemed to be bottomless.

Fast-forward a few years to when my team was conducting real-time fMRI neurofeedback experiments. As mentioned in the last chapter, I frequently acted as the guinea pig. I would climb into the scanner and meditate while Dustin, the graduate student, ran the controls. I remember one particular run when I decided to practice loving-kindness while watching a graph of my brain activity. I started by wishing well to Dustin and the scanner technologists in the control room. I started to feel warmth and an opening feeling in my chest. As I got warmed up, the expansive feeling took off. That description is the best that I can come up with—unbounded, full, warm. I wasn't

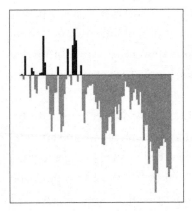

My brain on meditation. Graph showing my PCC brain activity while practicing loving-kindness meditation during pilot testing of our fMRI neurofeedback apparatus. Black indicates increased brain activity, and grey indicates decreased activity. Each bar represents a two-second measurement. The practice heated up in the middle (while my brain activity cooled down).

doing anything. It was just doing itself. And the sensation was very different from the type of giddy excitement I had felt during romance. It was more open. It didn't leave me wanting more. I looked up at the real-time feedback display after the three-minute test run. I could clearly see that about a third of the way in, my PCC activity decreased (corresponding to the dip below the horizontal line in the middle), and by the end of the run it had dropped significantly.

This result was great to see. We had already published a group-level analysis showing that, on average, PCC activity decreased during meditation. But there was something special about being able to see my brain activity line up so nicely with my experience during the practice of loving-kindness, which I had originally waved off as sappy.

After collecting much more data with novice and experienced meditators, we published our first paper mapping the changes in brain activity during loving-kindness meditation.[4] These data fit nicely with what we were learning about the role of the PCC in getting caught up in experience. When practicing loving-kindness in the scanner, experienced meditators uniformly reported the opposite of contracted excitement: warm, open, and so forth.

Our results also added a little piece to the puzzle of love. Previous reports had showed decreases in PCC activity in mothers and (nonobsessed) lovers, and our data confirmed that love doesn't necessarily have to activate brain regions associated with self-centeredness. Love doesn't have to be all about us. In fact, we might miss out on love's vast and deeply meaningful dimension if we try to make sure it is always centered on us.

These results were also congruent with Aron and Fisher's idea that increased PCC activity could mark a difference between being in love and being "addicted" to love. Interestingly, our study found that the reward pathways of the brain previously shown to become active during romantic love (and in studies of cocaine addicts) were notably quiet during loving-kindness practice. Might there be a unique neural signature of nonattached love? My experience, along with the fact that the Greeks had a separate word for it, supported the idea. And though still preliminary, our results hinted at it.

Fittingly, our paper on loving-kindness was published right before Valentine's Day.

PART TWO
Hitting Up Dopamine

• • •

7

Why Is It So Hard to Concentrate—or Is It?

The cure for boredom is curiosity. There is no cure for curiosity.

—*attributed to Dorothy Parker*

I have no special talents. I am only passionately curious.

—*Albert Einstein*

The ability to pay attention without becoming distracted is a core skill, whether we are raising children, building a business, developing a spiritual practice, or taking care of patients. In the medical field, one of the top complaints that patients lodge against doctors is that they aren't listening. Meditation is often touted as a straightforward way to develop this "mental muscle." Yet many of us who wade into these waters quickly return to shore, saying to ourselves, "This is too hard" or "I can't concentrate" or "How can this possibly be working? I feel worse."

In 1998, after finishing two years of both medical school and practicing mindfulness, I went on my first weeklong meditation retreat. A local teacher, Ginny Morgan, had rented a Catholic retreat center a little west of St. Louis. Ginny brought in a well-respected teacher named Bhante Gunaratana from his monastery in West Virginia. She was going to serve as the retreat manager for the week while he did the teaching. Having read Gunaratana's book *Mindfulness in Plain English*, I was excited to be able to learn from him (and also to see what it was like to hang out with a monk!).

The retreat offered a lot of silent meditation time but very little instruction. Gunaratana would sit unmoving in meditation posture for hours at the front of the sanctuary turned meditation hall, the rest of us arrayed in concentric semicircles around him. We were told that we could alternate between sitting and walking meditation at our own discretion. If we had questions, we could write them down, and he would answer them each evening when we were all assembled in the meditation hall—presumably so that we could learn from one another's queries.

About two days into the retreat, I found myself feeling defeated and depleted. I cried on Ginny's shoulder, choking out phrases such as "I can't do this" and "This is too hard." Gunaratana, who was seasoned in such matters, had even met with me one-on-one. He had given me suggestions such as "Start with counting the breaths up to seven" to help keep my mind still. The problem was that my mind would have none of it. No matter how much I tried, it could not be convinced that paying attention to my breath, of all things, was worth its time. And in retrospect, I can't blame it. Who would want to pay attention to a seemingly uninteresting, unexciting object like the breath when my mind was full of all sorts of better things—pleasant memories, exciting thoughts about future experiments, and so on. The choice between the two was a no-brainer for someone addicted to thinking.

Happiness?

In the early stages of meditation instruction, the emphasis is on paying attention to the breath, and returning one's attention to the breath when the mind has wandered. This practice is straightforward enough, but it runs counter to our natural reward-based mechanisms of learning. As discussed throughout this book, we learn best in some circumstances by pairing action with outcome. The Buddha taught this principle as well; he repeatedly admonished his followers to notice cause and effect, to see clearly what they were getting from their actions. In our lives today, what types of behaviors do we reinforce? It is likely that the majority of us do not reinforce ones that lead away from stress. As our stress compass may in fact be telling us (once we learn how to use it), we *are* actually looking for happiness in all the wrong places.

In 2008, I started reading more of the primary texts in the Pali Canon, such as those that described dependent origination (see chapter 1). As I read, I began to see that the Buddha was pointing out how we tend to lose our way while seeking happiness. Perhaps that observation was the basis for his radical statement on suffering and happiness: "What others call happiness, that the Noble Ones declare to be suffering. What others call suffering, that the Noble Ones have found to be happiness."[1] This same thought is likely what the Burmese teacher Sayadaw U Pandita was talking about when he said that we mistake excitement for happiness, even though the former disorients us and moves us toward suffering instead of away from it.

How did the Buddha know the difference between authentic happiness and suffering? First, he looked closely and observed basic reinforcement learning processes at work: "The more [people] indulge in sensual pleasures, the more their craving for sensual pleasures increases and the more they are burned by the fever of sensual pleasures, yet they find a certain measure of satisfaction and enjoyment in dependence on . . . sensual pleasure."[2] Behavior (indulgence in sensual pleasures) leads to reward (enjoyment), which sets up the process for its repetition (craving). If I spend an hour lost in one romantic fantasy after another, the excited feeling that I get from it leaves me craving more. The same thing happened to my patients when they drank or used drugs.

Interestingly, the Buddha followed this process of indulgence and intoxication to its end: "I set out seeking the gratification in the world. Whatever gratification there is in the world, that I have found. I have clearly seen with wisdom just how far the gratification in the world extends."[3] Historically, the Buddha was a prince. According to the story, when his mother became pregnant with him, many holy men gathered at the royal palace and prophesied that he would grow to be either a powerful monarch or a great spiritual leader. After hearing the prophesy, his father, the king, did everything in his power to ensure the former. He reasoned that if his son "was spared from all difficulty and heartache, the call to a spiritual destiny might remain dormant in him."[4] The king spoiled the young prince rotten, indulging his every desire and burying him in luxury.

Ironically, this sensible-seeming strategy may have backfired on the king. It wasn't until the Buddha had explored gratification to its end that he realized it didn't bring him lasting satisfaction—it simply left him wanting more. Contemplating this never-ending cycle, he woke up. He realized how the process worked and thus how to step out of it: "So long, monks, as I did not directly know, as they really are, the gratification in the world as gratification . . . I did not claim to have awakened to the unsurpassed perfect enlightenment in this world . . . But when I directly knew all this, then I claimed to have awakened. The knowledge and vision arose in me: 'Unshakeable is the liberation of my mind.'"[5]

In other words, it wasn't until he had seen clearly what he was actually getting from his actions—which actions led to happiness and which one perpetuated stress and suffering—that he could see how to change them. He learned how to read his stress compass. Once that happened, the way to reorient and move in a different direction was remarkably simple. It followed the basic principles of habit formation: if you drop the action that is causing stress, you will feel better immediately; in other words, pair behavior with reward, cause with effect. Importantly and perhaps paradoxically, dropping the action that causes stress comes about by simply being aware of what we are doing rather than by doing something to try to change or fix the situation. Instead of trying to get in there and untangle the snarled mess of our lives (and making it more tangled in the process), we step back and let it untangle itself. We move from doing into being.

When I read these passages in the Pali Canon, I had an "aha!" moment. These insights were important. Why? Because I had seen this cycle over and over again in my own experience—mistaking stress-inducing actions for ones that might give me (some) happiness, and repeating them anyway. I had seen it with my patients. And it lined up with modern theories of how we learn.

Seeing Is Believing

Sometime after my spar-with-your-thoughts retreat in 2006, I (finally) started watching what happened in my mind and body when I let my thought streams play themselves out instead of fighting or trying to control them. I started paying attention to cause and effect. And once I finished residency training, in 2008, I began attending longer and longer retreats so that I could really see what my mind was up to. It was on a monthlong retreat in 2009 that I truly began to understand that hamster wheel of dependent origination.

I was sitting in the meditation hall at a self-retreat center, watching different thoughts arise (cause), and noticing their effects in my body. My mind must not have been stimulated enough, because it started alternating between throwing sexual fantasies at me and fixating on my problems or worries. The pleasant fantasies led to an urge that I felt as a tightening and restlessness in my gut, or solar plexus area. I suddenly realized that the unpleasant worries *did the same thing.* For the first time in my life, I really saw how I was being sucked into my thoughts. And it didn't matter whether they were good or bad. Both kinds of thought streams ended with the same result: a restless craving that needed satisfying. I remember telling the retreat teachers about my "amazing discovery." They smiled politely, with a look that said, "Welcome to the club. Now you know where to start." And start I did. For the rest of that retreat, I explored gratification to its end, every chance I got. I watched thoughts arise, leading to urges for more thinking. I watched pleasant tastes arise during meals, leading to urges for more food. I watched restlessness arise during long sitting periods, leading to the urge to get up. As much as I could, I explored gratification to its end. I began to get a taste for disenchantment. The "seeing excitement as happiness" spell had been lifted. I started to understand how my stress compass worked. And that I had been mistakenly moving in the wrong direction, creating more suffering in the process.

Just as I had been doing by indulging in thought fantasies, most of us mistake suffering for happiness as we live our lives. How do we know? Because we haven't stopped perpetuating our suffering. Notice the number of times a day that we lash out at other people, eat comfort food, or buy something when stressed. Look at the ubiquitous advertisements promoting happiness through consumerism, feeding the concept that if we buy X, then we will be happy. These inducements work quite well because they take advantage of our innate reward-based learning processes: behavior leads to reward, which shapes and reinforces future behavior.

We have conditioned ourselves to deal with stress in ways that ultimately perpetuate it rather than release us from it.

The Buddha highlighted the misperception of stress for happiness: "In the same way . . . sensual pleasures in the past were painful to the touch, very hot & scorching; sensual pleasures in the future will be painful to the touch, very hot & scorching; sensual pleasures at present are painful to the touch, very hot & scorching; but when beings are not free from passion for sensual pleasures—devoured by sensual craving, burning with sensual fever—their faculties are impaired, which is why, even though sensual pleasures are actually painful to the touch, they have the skewed perception of 'pleasant.' "[6] This false identification is what my patients deal with daily. They don't know how to use their stress compass. The short-term rewards from smoking or doing drugs lead them in the wrong direction. And we do the same thing by stress eating instead of stopping when we are full, or by binge-watching a television series on Netflix instead of pacing ourselves.

If reward-based learning is our natural tendency, why not co-opt it to learn how to move from temporary "happiness" to lasting states of peace, contentment, and joy? In fact, why aren't we doing this already?

B. F. Skinner argued that reward is critical for changing behavior: "Behavior could be changed by changing its consequences—that was operant conditioning—but it could be changed because other kinds of consequences would then follow."[7] Is it possible that we *don't even need to change the consequences* (rewards), as Skinner suggested? If we simply see what we are getting from our actions more clearly, the cost of current consequences becomes more apparent. In other words, rewards may not be as juicy as we think they are when we stop long enough to actually taste them. The fourteenth-century Persian mystic and poet, Hafiz (Hafez) captured this truth in a poem entitled "And Applaud":

Once a young man came to me and said,

"Dear Master,
I am feeling strong and brave today,
And I would like to know the truth
About all of my—attachments."

And I replied,

"Attachments?
Attachments!

Sweet Heart,
Do you really want me to speak to you
About all your attachments,

When I can see so clearly
You have built, with so much care,
Such a great brothel
To house all of your pleasures.

You have even surrounded the whole damn place
With armed guards and vicious dogs
To protect your desires

So that you can sneak away
From time to time

And try to squeeze light
Into your parched being
From a source as fruitful
As a dried date pit
That even a bird
Is wise enough to spit out.[8]

Until we define happiness for ourselves, clearly seeing the difference between excitement and joy, for example, our habits will likely not change. We will keep returning to the fruits of our desires.

From Lemons to Lemonade

One of the early discourses in the Pali Canon is entitled *Anapanasati Sutta,* which concerns the mindfulness of breathing. The sutta starts with instructions on breath awareness: "Always mindful, he breathes in; mindful he breathes out."[9] It continues, "Breathing in long, he discerns, 'I am breathing in long'; or breathing out long, he discerns, 'I am breathing out long,'" and then continues with a list of things to progress to, including the entire body, pleasure, and even making things up in our heads, translated as "mental fabrication." It seems that many teachers may stop at the breath. That was certainly what I had learned, and trying to stay with my breath had kept me quite occupied for many years.

Later in the same sutta is a list of the "seven factors of awakening." They are as follows: mindfulness (Pali: *sati*), interest/investigation (*dhamma vicaya*), courageous energy (*viriya*), joy/rapture (*piti*), tranquility/relaxation (*passaddhi*), concentration (*samadhi*), and equanimity (*upekkha*).[10]

Perhaps just as important as the list itself is the order of the items on it. Returning to cause-and-effect models, the Buddha argued that as we try to move away from suffering and become mindful of present-moment experience, an interest in seeing cause and effect naturally arises. If the goal is to reduce or end our stress, we need simply to direct our attention to our experience, and the interest in seeing whether we are increasing or decreasing stress in that moment naturally arises as a result. We do not have to do anything but look. This process is like reading a good book. If we want to read it, we begin reading, and assuming the book is good, we become interested in continuing to read. This parallels mindfulness practice, since we have to truly and wholeheartedly *want* to stop suffering. Otherwise, we will not look at our actions carefully enough to see what we are actually getting from them. As we start to get into the book, the energy to keep reading naturally arises. So too with mindfulness practice—we become more interested in investigating more and more what we are doing. We can ask ourselves, "What am I getting from this? Is it leading me toward or away from suffering?" When the book gets really good, we become enraptured, perhaps finding ourselves reading until three in the morning. Once enraptured, we can tranquilly sit and read for hours.

At this point, we really start to concentrate. With the previous factors in place, concentration naturally arises—we don't have to force it or keep returning to the object of focus from daydreams or other distractions. This was not how I first learned to concentrate. Pay attention, and when the mind wanders, bring it back. Repeat. Here the sutta specifically emphasizes the use of cause and effect. Create the conditions for X, and X will naturally arise.

Rub the sticks of mindfulness and interest together, and five steps later concentration will naturally arise as the fire gets going. Forcing concentration is really difficult, as anyone knows from experience, whether we are studying for a licensing exam or trying to stay tuned in while our spouse talks about something less exciting than our Facebook feed. We know all too well how hard it is to concentrate when we are restless. Once we learn to concentrate, the conditions for equanimity naturally arise. Reading a good book on the subway is not a problem when we achieve equanimity; no matter the commotion around us, we are unflappable.

When trying to concentrate on an object, whether it is our breath, a conversation, or something else, how do we make that state our new default way of being? How do we clearly see what we are getting—what reward—from our behavior in any moment? Perhaps we start at the beginning by simply noticing what it feels like when something interests us or draws our curiosity—or even fascinates us. For me, there is an open, energized, joyful quality in being really curious. That feeling clearly defines the reward that results from bringing the first two factors of awakening together: mindfulness and interest. We can contrast that experience with moments when we felt some type of brief, excited "happiness" that came from getting something that we wanted. When I set up my engagement scavenger hunt for Mary, I mistook the resulting excitement for happiness. Only years later did the difference become clear to me. Excitement brings with it restlessness and a contracted urge for more. Joy that results from curiosity is smoother, and open rather than contracted.

The critical distinction between these types of rewards is that joy arises from being attentive and curious. That type of consciousness is possible virtually at any waking moment. It doesn't take any work— since awareness is always available, we can simply rest in *being* aware. Excitement, on the other hand, requires something to happen to us or requires us to procure something that we want—we have to *do* something to get what we want. To start switching from excitement to joyful engagement, we can notice triggers (stress), perform a behavior (drop into an open, curious awareness), and notice the rewards (joy, tranquility, equanimity). And by using our own reward-based learning processes, the more we take these steps, the more we set up a habit pattern to concentrate more deeply and be happier (in a nonexcited way). In fact, we might discover that that this mode of being is always available, given the right conditions, such as getting out of our own way.

The Brain on Curiosity

It may seem counterintuitive or paradoxical to think that we can use our own reward-based habit-learning systems to move beyond addiction or the excited type of reward-based happiness.

How can we become interested to the point of becoming fascinated and enraptured? How can we differentiate being joyfully curious from being selfishly excited? In other words, how can we tell whether we are on the right track when practicing? The short answer here is that it can be tricky to tell the difference between joy (selfless) and excitement (selfish), especially early in mindfulness training, when we may not have had experience with selfless modes of being. And of course, we move ourselves away from these the more we *try* to achieve them. If we have access to a neuroscience laboratory, perhaps we can peek into our brains to see which regions become more or less active when we become interested in an object. For instance, what do regions of the brain implicated in self-referential processing do when we pay attention to our breath?

For example, we put a novice meditator in the fMRI scanner in my lab and gave her the standard breath awareness instruction: "Pay attention to the physical sensation of the breath wherever you feel it most strongly in the body, and follow the natural and spontaneous movement of the breath, not trying to change it in any way." Subsequently—and not surprisingly, given my own experience during the first decade of practice—she reported relative difficulty in concentrating. We were measuring the activity in her posterior cingulate cortex. Like participants in our other studies, she reported a strong correlation between her subjective experience of difficulty in concentrating and increased brain activity pattern, especially at the end of the run

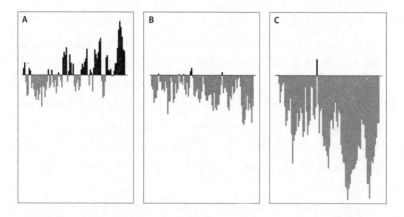

Examples of fMRI brain activity change in the PCC. *A,* a novice meditator who was instructed to pay attention to the breath; *B,* an experienced meditator who was instructed to pay attention to the breath; C, an experienced meditator who was instructed to pay attention to the breath, and in particular to any related feeling of interest, wonder, and joy. Increases in brain activity relative to baseline are indicated by increases in the graph above the horizontal bar (black), and decreases are below the bar (grey). Each meditation period lasted three minutes. Reproduced from J. A. Brewer, J. H. Davis, and J. Goldstein, "Why Is It So Hard to Pay Attention, or Is It? Mindfulness, the Factors of Awakening, and Reward-Based Learning," *Mindfulness* 4, no. 1 (2013): 75–80. Copyright Springer Science+Business Media, New York, 2012. Used with permission.

(see figure, part a). We then gave an experienced meditator the same instructions. As expected, his PCC activity was consistently decreased relative to baseline (figure, part b). Interestingly, when another experienced meditator practiced "focusing on his breath and *in particular the feeling of interest, wonder, and joy* that arose in conjunction with subtle, mindful breathing," he showed a large drop in the relative activation of the PCC, which correlated with his experience of "feeling interested and joy," even when "being curious about the draft on [his] hands and feet" (figure, part c).

Though these are examples of a single brain region that is likely part of a larger network contributing to these experiences, they suggest that creating the right conditions for concentration, including curiosity, may be helpful in "not feeding" self-referential processes. In the future, giving this type of neurofeedback to people while they are practicing may be helpful in differentiating practice that is selfish from that which is selfless, excited from joyful, and contracted from open, similar to what I experienced when practicing loving-kindness in the scanner.

When it comes to staying focused, we may be able to treat mind states or attitudes such as curiosity as conditions that can naturally lead to concentration. If so, we could abandon brute force methods that may not be as clearly linked with our natural reward-based learning processes. These tools and skills may be *inherent* in reward-based learning. If so, we can leverage them to change our lives without the usual roll-up-your-sleeves, no-pain-no-gain, effortful methodology that seems baked into our Western psyche. Before I came to this realization, I was using the techniques that I knew best, which, ironically, were moving me in the wrong direction. Instead, we can notice the trigger (stress), perform the behavior (become interested and curious), and reward ourselves in a way that is aligned with our stress compass (notice joy, tranquility, concentration, and equanimity). Repeat.

Or as the poet Mary Oliver put it:

Instructions for living a life:
Pay attention.
Be astonished.
Tell about it.[11]

8

Learning to Be Mean—and Nice

When I do good, I feel good, when I do bad, I feel bad, and
that is my religion.

—*Abraham Lincoln*

Yik Yak, a social media app developed by Tyler Droll and Brooks
Buffington, allows people to anonymously create and view discussion
threads within a certain radius of their phones. According to the
company's blog, six months after it was released in 2013, Yik Yak was
the ninth most downloaded social media app in the United States.
What makes it so popular? The splash screen of the app says it
all: "Get a live feed of what people are saying around you. Upvote
what's good & downvote what's not. No profiles, no passwords, it's all
anonymous." In a *New York Times* article titled "Who Spewed That
Abuse? Anonymous Yik Yak App Isn't Telling," Jonathan Mahler described something that happened in an honors class at Eastern Mich-
igan University: "While the professors [three women] had been lec-
turing about post-apocalyptic culture, some of the 230 or so freshmen
in the auditorium had been having a separate conversation about
them on a social media site called Yik Yak. There were dozens of posts,
most demeaning, many using crude, sexually explicit language and
imagery."[1]

While these students were supposed to be learning about a particular kind of culture, they were taking part in a different one, an app culture shaped by rewards that come in the form of points or other shiny objects, à la Skinner, instead of from direct interaction with others. The Yik Yak website is not shy in pointing this out: "Earn Yakarma points. Get rewarded for posting awesome Yaks!" Perhaps more rewarding than getting gold stars is the chance to gossip, which has the same ripe feel as other types of excitement—hence the term "juicy gossip." We sit in a college lecture hall, our phones in our laps, and suddenly see them spring to life with a funny post. With that unexpected stimulus, we get a spritz of dopamine. Then we can't sit still as our minds swirl with excitement, trying to outdo the previous post. All this activity is safe (for us) because it is anonymous. As Jordan Seman, a sophomore at Middlebury College, said in Mahler's *New York Times* article, "It's so easy for anyone in any emotional state to post something, whether that person is drunk or depressed or wants to get revenge on someone. And then there are no consequences."

We all can remember back to our childhoods and perhaps even recall the face of a schoolyard or classroom bully. Yet usually there was only one or two. Has the anonymity and the scaling of social media spawned a rash of self-centered cyberbullies? In an interview with the television talk show host Conan O'Brien (September 20, 2013), the comedian Louis C.K. made an astute observation about smartphones:

> You know, I think these things are toxic, especially for kids. It's this thing. It's bad. They don't look at people when they talk to them. They don't build the empathy. Kids are mean, and it's because they're trying it out. They look at a kid and they go, you're fat. Then they see the kid's face scrunch up and say ooh, that doesn't feel good. But when they write

[in a text message on their phone] they're fat, they go, hmm, that was fun.

In chapter 2, we looked at the compelling nature of mobile devices, and the ease with which they can hook us by reinforcing, in several ways, self-centered actions such as posting selfies or self-disclosing. But Louis C.K. seems to be getting at something else here. Certain features of smartphone technology, such as an absence of face-to-face contact, may be affecting our lives in ways that fundamentally shape how we learn to interact with others. Anonymous social media apps may be the stickiest. Following simple Skinnerian principles, they provide all the juice of a reward, but without any accountability (negative reinforcement). In turn, since we cannot accurately assess the full results of our actions, we become subjectively biased to increasingly look for this type of reward and to look away from any damage that we might be causing.

In Skinner's preface to *Walden Two,* he wrote, "Good personal relations also depend upon immediate signs of condemnation or censure, supported perhaps by simple rules or codes" (xi). High schools can punish students for bullying, and social media apps can limit technology use, yet these types of rules may just spur rebellious teenagers on. Remember: immediacy of reward is important for reward-based learning. We get immediate rewards (Yakarma points) when our Yik Yak posts get upvoted. Punishment in the form of school suspension or something similar comes long after the reward has been reaped. And forbidding the use of apps falls into the category of cognitive (or other types of) control—even if we know that we shouldn't have our phones on during lectures, at moments of weakness, addicted to that buzz of excitement that comes with gossip, we can't seem to help ourselves.

In pointing to the principles of reward-based learning, Skinner may have been suggesting codes different from those now in place. He argued that for punishments to work—to be correctly associated with an action—they too had to be immediate. For example, how many of us have friends who, when their parents caught them smoking, immediately made them smoke ten cigarettes? Since nicotine is a toxin, the more we smoke cigarette after cigarette before our bodies have had a chance to build up a tolerance to them, the more they signal, "Toxic behavior! Abort! Abort!" We feel nauseated and vomit (often repeatedly) as our body strongly signals for us to stop doing whatever we are doing.

Lucky for us and our parents! If the association with that punishment sticks, the next time we see a cigarette, we might feel nauseated—a warning as our body anticipates what will happen if we smoke it. Similarly, Antabuse, a drug treatment for alcoholism, causes effects resembling something akin to an instant hangover. And we can imagine instituting immediate punishments for cyberbullying and malicious gossip. Yet, is creating additional codes, whether blanket rules or immediate punishments, the best way forward?

(Self-) Righteous Anger

In 2010, I went on a monthlong silent retreat with the aim of working on and possibly stabilizing a specific concentration type of meditation practice (*jhana*) that can be held for hours if practiced correctly. I had been reading about and trying to develop this practice for the past two years under the wise eye of my teacher, Joseph Goldstein. As with other types of concentration, one needs to set up the conditions that will allow jhanic states to arise. Reportedly, one of these conditions was to remove or temporarily suspend mind states, or "hindrances," that could get in the way, including pleasant fantasies and anger. This made sense to me. As I had seen on my retreat the previous year, each time I got caught up in either daydreams or angry thoughts, I was, well, caught up in myself and estranged from the object of concentration. Reportedly, jhanic practice was even more sensitive to these hindrances. One slight misstep, and one would fall into old habitual patterns and then have to re-create the conditions from scratch.

At the time of my retreat, I had been dealing with some challenges at work. I had a colleague, "Jane," with whom I was having some difficulty. Details aside (yes, gossip is juicy!), let's just say I became angry whenever I thought of her. I kept a journal on each retreat, and at the beginning of this particular one, I wrote about Jane daily (often with underlined phrases). Here I was on retreat in a quiet, beautiful setting. All the physical conditions were perfect for me to concentrate. Yet my mental conditions were a mess. Each time a thought of her arose in my mind, I would cycle through endless mental simulations in which I would do this or that, all the while getting angrier and angrier. Of course, because these were my simulations, I was justified in being angry, because of the way Jane had treated *me,* and the things that she wanted *from me,* and so on. It would take me forever to climb out of the pit, and even longer to calm down.

This predicament reminded me of one of the passages from the Pali Canon: "Whatever a [person] frequently thinks and ponders upon, that will become the inclination of his mind."[2] As Skinner might have said, anger was now my habit. I was just spinning my wheels, and all the while sinking deeper and deeper in the sand.

On my third day of retreat, I came up with a word that I would say to myself as a reminder that I was getting caught up and about to fall into the pit, and needed to regain my balance quickly. It was "big." Big. Big. Big. For me, "big" meant to remember to open my heart big and wide when I started closing down with anger. Soon thereafter, during a walking meditation period, I again got lost in an angry fantasy. This mind state had a very seductive quality to it; anger is described in the Dhammapada, a Buddhist scripture, as having a "poisoned root and honeyed tip." I asked myself, "What am I getting from this?" What reward had I been giving myself so often that I was constantly in this pit? The answer came in a blaze: *nothing!* Anger, with its poisoned root and honeyed tip indeed!

This was perhaps the first time that I really saw that getting caught up in self-righteous, self-referential thinking served as its own reward. Like my smokers who realized that smoking really didn't taste good, I finally saw that my contraction "buzz" from getting all high and mighty with anger was just perpetuating itself. I needed to heed Confucius's advice: "Before you embark on a journey of revenge, dig two graves."

Once I clearly saw that instead of getting anywhere near my goal of concentration meditation on this retreat, I was merely going around and around with anger, something lifted. Like my patients who started to become disenchanted with smoking, I started to become disenchanted with anger. Each time I saw it arise, it was less and less of a struggle to let go of it, because I could taste its poison, immediately. I didn't need to have someone hit me with a stick and say, "Stop getting angry!" Simply seeing it was enough to allow me to let go of it. I am not claiming that I never got angry again on the retreat or that I don't get angry now. When I do, I just get less excited about it. Its rewarding properties are gone. And this change is very interesting if we look at it from the perspective of reward-based learning.

Returning to the idea that we learn from rewards and punishments: is it possible that instead of meting out punishments for "bad behavior"—and such consequences would have to be immediate in order to work most effectively—there may be an alternate strategy for success? Louis C.K. pointed out something important about kids using smartphones: "Kids are mean, and it's because they're trying it out. They look at a kid and they go, you're fat. Then they see the kid's face scrunch up and say ooh, that doesn't feel good. But when they write they're fat, they go, hmm, that was fun." There may be plenty of punishment in simply seeing the results of our actions: if they cause harm and we see that they do, we will be less excited to repeat them in the future. As I saw with getting caught up in anger while on retreat, we would become disenchanted with harmful actions. Why? Because they hurt. But it is critical that we actually and accurately see what is happening. Mindfulness can be extremely helpful in this regard. We must remove our glasses of subjective bias, which skew how we interpret what is happening ("hmm, that was fun"), so that we can clearly see everything that results from our behavior. Unless we get that immediate feedback—seeing the consequences of our actions—we may learn something else entirely.

Turning the Tables

I discussed the possibility of reward-based learning extending into the realm of ethical behavior with my friend the philosopher Jake Davis. It seemed like the right conversation to have with a former monk who, while living as a monastic, followed a code of daily living (*vinaya*). How many rules did they have? In the Theravada tradition there are more than two hundred rules for monks and more than three hundred for nuns (a notable difference). He agreed that it would be interesting to explore ethics as learned behavior. He started looking into it, and a few years later he was awarded his PhD after successfully defending his 165-page dissertation, entitled "Acting Wide Awake: Attention and the Ethics of Emotion."[3]

Jake's paper moves away from moral relativism, a view that moral judgments are true or false only relative to a particular standpoint (such as that of a culture or a historical period). For an example of this type of relativism, he uses the case of "honor killings" of young women who have been raped. Some may consider the practice immoral, while others might feel strongly that such traditional killings are necessary to save the honor of a family. Instead of relying on relativism, Jake takes into account individual emotional motivations as the focus of ethical evaluation. He phrased it thus, "Does how we feel about *how we feel* about things matter ethically?" (emphasis added). In other words, might reward-based learning converge with mindfulness (in this case, Buddhist ethics) to provide individual situational ethics? Can we derive ethical decisions from seeing the results of our actions? Through the rest of his thesis, Jake explores several ethical frameworks, including Philippa Foot's Aristotelian account, John Stuart Mill's utilitarianism, the theories of Immanuel Kant and David Hume, and even hedonism. He compares how all these views stack up from a philosophical viewpoint, pointing out potential limitations.

Jake then discusses evidence from modern psychology. Why is it that in certain situations, we would rather lose money to punish someone else if we feel that he or she is being unfair to us? A game used in moral research studies called the Ultimatum Game is set up to specifically test this tendency. Participant A (usually a computer algorithm, but often portrayed as a real person) offers to share a certain amount of money with participant B (the true subject of the experiment). Participant B decides whether to accept or reject the proposed division of funds. If B rejects the offer, neither participant gets any money. After testing multiple scenarios and calculating which types of offers B will accept or reject, a set point for fairness can be determined. In such games, people report increases in emotions like anger and disgust when they feel that the other side is not "playing fair."[4]

But meditators behave more altruistically in these scenarios, willingly accepting more unfair offers than nonmeditators.[5] Ulrich Kirk and colleagues provided some insight into this phenomenon by measuring participants' brain activity while they were playing the Ultimatum Game. They looked at the anterior insula, a brain region linked to awareness of body states, emotional reactions (for example, disgust) in particular. Activity in this region has been shown to predict whether an unfair offer will be rejected.[6] Kirk found that meditators showed decreased activity in the anterior insula compared to nonmeditators. The researchers suggested that this lower degree of activation "enabled them to uncouple negative emotional reactions from their behavior." Perhaps they could more easily see their emotions arising and clouding their judgment (that is, leading them to fall into the "fairness" subjective bias), and by seeing the lack of inherent reward in punishing the other participant, they decided not to follow through on the behavior. They could step out of the "I'm going to stick it to you!" habit loop because it wasn't as rewarding for them as other responses. As Jake puts it in his dissertation, "The costs of retributive response may indeed outweigh the benefits." Fairness aside, it is more painful to be a jerk than to be nice to one.

Jake concludes that we may indeed learn ethical values that are based on (and subjectively biased toward) cultural and situational norms. Grounding his arguments in behavioral psychology and neurobiology, he asserts that "by appealing to ethical judgments that all members of our human moral community would make if they were alert and unbiased, we can make sense of the idea that individuals and groups sometimes get the normative truth wrong, and that we sometimes get it right." In other words, being able to see our subjective biases, which are born from our previous reactions, may be enough to help us learn a common human ethic.

Stephen Batchelor seems to agree. In *After Buddhism,* he writes that the development of awareness "entails a fundamental realignment of one's sensitivity to the feelings, needs, longings and fears of others." He continues, "Mindfulness means empathizing with the condition and plight of others as revealed through an enhanced 'reading' of their bodies." In other words, it helps to see clearly. He concludes that this clarity is important for disrupting "innate tendencies of egoism," which in turn contributes to "letting go of self-interested reactivity."[7] If we can take off our blur-inducing glasses of self-focus and subjective bias, which lead us to *habitually react* to the world through fear, anger, and so forth, we will be able to see the results of our actions more clearly (by getting a better read from others' body language), and we may respond more skillfully to each moment's unique circumstances.

Bringing fuller awareness to our encounters may help us move beyond blanket codes of conduct derived from such questions as "Why do I have to?" and "How does this apply to me?" Seeing the reaction on someone's face when we call them fat may silently speak volumes: "This is why." As children grow up learning the results of their behavior, they might broaden their application of the "don't be mean" rule to cover a wide range of moral decisions rather than immediately searching for loopholes or ways to circumvent externally imposed restrictions (an idea that may apply especially to teens and young adults). If we follow our biology—how we have evolved to learn—and simply start paying attention to what our bodies are telling us, the rules might get simpler (though not necessarily easier). Get triggered. Be a jerk. See how much pain this causes both parties. Don't repeat.

Giving Feels Good

For those of us who get fired up when we see injustices in the world, righteous anger might seem to be a good thing. We may feel that getting up off the couch as we shake our fist at a politician giving a speech will motivate us to vote. Watching YouTube videos of police brutality may motivate us to join an advocacy group or do some community organizing. We may also wonder what would happen if we didn't get angry. Would we just sit on the couch like a lump?

On my "anger" meditation retreat, I noticed that my habit was not helping me concentrate. I started to become less excited about it (disenchanted) and noticed that, as a result, I freed up a lot more energy for other things. Why? As probably all of us can attest, anger is *exhausting!* On my retreat, this repurposed energy went toward the development of a less distracted and, yes, much more concentrated mind. As the distraction of anger died down, I was able to bring the proper conditions together to drop into a very concentrated state—one that stayed on point for up to an hour at a time. That was a welcome change.

One of the factors that I mentioned in the last chapter that is needed for concentration is joy. Again, not agitated, restless excitement, but a joy that feels expansive and tranquil. Since anger and anticipatory excitement move us in the opposite direction, we need to find which types of activities foster joyful states.

At some point in my meditation training, I learned a three-step "graduated" teaching that was part of Theravada Buddhism. It started with generosity, moved to virtuous conduct, and then, only after those had been practiced did one advance to mental development, as in meditation. The relevant insight from tradition and experience boils down to this: if you go around all day acting like a jerk, it will be hard to sit down and meditate. Why? Because as soon as we try to focus on an object, everything that was emotionally charged from the day will come marching into our heads, making it impossible to concentrate. If we come to the cushion not having lied, cheated, or stolen, there is "less garbage to take out" as Leigh Brasington, a meditation teacher specializing in concentration practices, likes to say. If this kind of virtuous conduct is the *second* step, what about the first, generosity?

What does it feel like when we are generous? It feels good, an open, joyful state. Practicing generosity may help us learn what it feels like to let go. We are literally letting go when we give someone a gift. Yet not all generosity is equal. What happens when we give a gift and expect something in return? Does it feel joyful to donate a large sum of money with the expectation of receiving some type of recognition? What kind of satisfaction do we get when we hold the door for our boss or a date with the intention of impressing her or him? In an essay entitled "No Strings Attached: The Buddha's Culture of Generosity," Thanissaro Bhikkhu highlighted a passage in the Pali Canon listing three factors that exemplified the ideal gift: "The donor, before giving, is glad; while giving, his/her mind is inspired; and after giving, is gratified."[8] That sequence sounds much like reward-based learning. The donor is glad (trigger); while giving, her mind is inspired (behavior); and after giving, she feels gratified (reward).

Let's look at the holding-the-door scenario in two ways. We are on our first date with someone and want to make a good impression. We go out of our way to hold the door. If we are hoping to get some signal that we are doing a good job (reward), we might expect the door holding to garner a "thanks" or "you're so thoughtful" or at least a nod of appreciation. If we don't get that nod, it doesn't feel so good. We expected something and didn't get it. In particular, this lack of recognition can explain the burnout experienced by those who constantly help others but return home exhausted, feeling unappreciated—like modern martyrs.

On the other hand, if we selflessly hold the door, what would we expect? Absolutely nothing. Because we weren't looking for a reward. It wouldn't matter whether our date thanked us or not. Yet holding the door would still feel good, because the act provides an intrinsic reward. Giving feels good, especially when untainted by an expectation of recognition on the back end—no strings attached. That condition may be what the passage in the Pali Canon is pointing to. When we selflessly give, we don't have to worry about buyer's remorse because we aren't buying anything. This intrinsic reward leaves us feeling gratified and lays down a memory that prompts us to do the same thing the next time. Plenty of scientific studies have shown the health and wellness benefits of generosity. Instead of my describing all the details of that work in order to convince you, why not try the experiment yourself? You can do it without an fMRI scanner or a double-blind experimental design. The next time you hold the door for someone, see whether there is a difference in your felt experience of happiness (joy, warmth, and so forth) between holding it with an expectation of reward and holding it selflessly. Did the results help you learn how to properly read your stress compass—what types of rewards orient you toward or away from stress?

9

On Flow

Your me is in the way.

—*attributed to Hui Hai*

My mom put a lock on our television set when I was growing up. She installed a kill switch on our TV's power supply, to which only she had the key. My dad left when I was six, and my mother was at work a lot, raising four children on her own. After school and during the summers, without nudges in another direction, we could have easily been drawn in by the mesmerizing glow of cartoons or adventure shows. It was easy to be triggered simply by walking by the TV and then get rewarded with a pleasant-feeling dullness—a mental escape into the fantasies and lives portrayed by others in front of a camera. She didn't want us to grow up watching the "boob tube," as she put it, becoming addicted to television. She wanted us to find other, more interesting, less mindless (and addictive) things to do. Since the average American watches four hours of television *each* day, I thank her for what she did.

My mom's padlock forced me outdoors, where I learned to entertain myself. There I found the bicycle. In junior high school, my friend Charlie and I spent endless hours either riding or fixing up our BMX bikes. We spent our paper route money on new parts, and we washed our bikes anytime they had even a little dirt on them. Not too far from our neighborhood, a wooded expanse had dirt trails with ramps and the more challenging double jumps, an up and a down ramp. On the double jumps, our speed and timing had to be perfect. If we didn't get enough speed, we would crash into the lip of the down ramp. If we had too much speed, we would overshoot the mark. We rode those trails as much as we could, endlessly racing each other and practicing our jumps.

Growing up in Indianapolis, Charlie and I were lucky enough to be near the Major Taylor Velodrome. The velodrome was an open-air circular track where grown-ups could race fixed-gear track bikes. Next to the track was a bona fide BMX dirt track that we got to use. It had banked turns (dirt, of course) as well as huge ramps, "tabletop" jumps, and even triple jumps! Our mothers would take us there to race on weekends in the summer.

When I went off to college, mountain bikes were coming on the scene. I bought one during my freshman year and rode it every-where—on campus and on the local mountain bike trails with friends. In medical school, I bought my first bike with front suspension, which allowed me to ride on more challenging terrain. There were excellent trails within an hour of St. Louis, and each medical school class had enthusiasts that I could link up with (school was challenging, but we would always find time to get out for a ride). In the summers, I started traveling with friends to places that had "real" mountain biking, like Colorado and Wyoming. We rode huge descents in Durango and long stretches of single track in Alaska's Kenai Peninsula. On these big trips, we judged our rides by how "epic" they were.

And that was when I started tripping into flow. Flow is at the opposite end of the spectrum from habit. Mindlessly watching TV or automatically saying, "I'm fine; how are you?" when someone greets us are examples of responses that are triggered by a stimulus, yet are disengaged. We can feel as if we are on autopilot, almost floating somewhere (but don't know where), with a daydreamy, spaced-out quality of awareness. In contrast, awareness during flow experiences is vivid, bright, and engaged. We are *here:* so close to the camera, so engaged with the action, that we forget we are separate from it. I didn't have a language for it at the time, but that feeling of completely losing myself in a mountain bike ride was directly related to how epic I judged it to be afterward. Although I had experienced transcendent moments while making music in college, I had chalked it up to what happened when my quartet or orchestra played well together. But on the bike, I was having these flow moments more and more regularly.

Getting Our Flow On

The psychologist Mihály Csíkszentmihályi coined the term "flow" in the 1970s while studying why people were willing to give up material goods for "the elusive experience of performing enjoyable acts" such as rock climbing.[1] It became his life's work to define how we conceptualize "being in the zone." In an interview with *Wired* magazine, he described flow as "being completely involved in an activity for its own sake." When that happens, wonderful things occur: "The ego falls away. Time flies. Every action, movement, and thought follows inevitably from the previous one, like playing jazz."[2]

Elements of flow include the following:

☐ Concentration being focused and grounded in the present moment
☐ The merging of action and awareness
☐ A loss of reflective self-consciousness (for example, self-evaluation)

- ☐ A sense that one can deal with whatever arises in a given situation because one's "practice" has become a form of implicit embodied knowledge
- ☐ One's subjective experience of time becoming altered so that the "present" is continuously unfolding
- ☐ An experience of the activity as intrinsically rewarding[3]

At times when I was mountain biking, I would sometimes lose all sense of myself, the bike, and the environment. It wasn't zoning out; it was more like zoning in. Everything would simply merge into this amazing fusion of awareness and action. I wasn't there, yet there I was, in some of the most awesome experiences of my life. The best way I can describe moments like this is that they were delicious.

We all have experienced flow at one point or another. We get absorbed in something that we are doing—playing a sport, playing or listening to music, working on a project. When we look up from what we have been doing, it is five hours later and dark outside, and our bladder is about to explode—we were so focused we didn't notice. It would be great if we could produce this experience on demand.

The more often I experienced flow, the more I could recognize afterward the conditions that had increased the likelihood of it arising during that ride. After a year or so of being able to access flow, I started to put on my scientific hat and look at my experiences to identify these conditions and see whether I could reproduce them.

Book after book (for example, Steven Kotler's *The Rise of Superman*, published in 2014) has described the epic adventures of "flow junkies," extreme sportsmen and sportswomen who risk life and limb to chase the perfect high—yes, flow too can be addictive. Many authors have tried to find the secret ingredients, often pumping athletes and other flow junkies for information. In 2014, Dean Potter, a record-setting extreme sports athlete who had often spoken of flow, was interviewed by the documentary filmmaker Jimmy Chin:

JIMMY: You enjoy a variety of pretty intense activities: BASE-jumping, slacklining, free-soloing. What's the common thread here, besides the adrenaline piece?

DEAN: The common thread in my 3-Arts is pushing into fear, exhaustion, beauty and the unknown. I willingly expose myself to death-consequence situations in order to predictably enter heightened awareness. In times when I'm going to die if I mess up, my senses peak in order to survive, and I see, hear, feel, intuit in vast detail, beyond my normal, day-to-day consciousness. This pursuit of heightened awareness is why I put myself in harm's way.

In addition, while doing my arts, I empty myself and function within a meditative state where I focus on nothing but my breathing. This manifests emptiness. This void needs to be filled, and somehow it draws in and makes me recognize the roots of my most meaningful ponderings and often leads to a feeling of connectivity with everything.[4]

Tragically, Potter died in 2015 while performing one of his arts: BASE jumping from a cliff in Yosemite.

What Potter observed is that certain predictable conditions create flow. One of them seems to be extreme danger. When we are in a dangerous situation, we don't have time to think about ourselves. We focus on keeping "us" alive; afterward, the self comes back online and freaks out like a concerned parent—*that was really dangerous, you could have gotten hurt, don't ever do that again.* I can clearly remember once when this happened to me. On a backcountry skiing trip, I had to traverse a very steep and crumbly snowbank just above a raging river (which flowed right into a frozen lake). I was wearing a heavy mountaineering backpack with a week's worth of food and gear in it. Not being a good skier, I took off my Telemark skis and used them as anchors to help support my weight as I kick-stepped across the traverse. Kick, plant. Kick, plant. Kick, plant. When I had safely made it across, I looked around and started summing up the scene. A huge rush of adrenaline hit me, along with a voice screaming in my head, "You could have died!" Focus first. Worry later.

Although researchers have debated for decades about what it takes to get into a flow experience and stay there, there is no consensus on how to reliably reproduce this state in controlled environments, or on what brain activation (or deactivation) and neurotransmitters are involved in it. Near-death experiences are not conditions that we want to test in the lab.

Are there other clues about (less dangerous) conditions that support flow? Csíkszentmihályi emphasized that a balance must be struck between the difficulty of the task and the skill of the performer. What was he getting at? Pondering this question of balance after mountain bike rides, I started to understand what it meant. When I rode on flat, unchallenging terrain, my mind was likely to chatter away. If I tried to do something that was too technical for me at the time, I would fall or stop frequently (and get frustrated with myself). Yet when the conditions were perfect—riding on terrain that was challenging enough not to be boring, yet not too challenging—I was much more likely to pop into flow.

From a brain perspective, this idea of balance fits with what we currently know about self-referential networks. The default mode network gets quiet when someone concentrates on a task, but lights up in circumstances that promote boredom. In addition, it is activated during self-evaluation and other types of self-reference. And of course, the DMN gets really quiet during meditation. DMN deactivation may correspond to the "loss of reflective self-consciousness" that Csíkszentmihályi referred to.

Relatedly, many of the other elements of flow sound surprisingly similar to aspects of meditation: Concentration focused and grounded in the present moment. Subjective experience of a continuously unfolding "present" moment. Intrinsic reward. As we have explored throughout this book, these descriptors apply to mindfulness, too, whether we are in formal meditation or just being mindful as we go about the day. When we get out of our own way and into the momentary flow of life, it feels pretty good. Not surprisingly, Csíkszentmihályi even mentioned meditation as a way to train flow.

What about joy and flow? In the last chapter, we saw that joy can arise as a result of being generous, another manifestation of moving away from a focus on ourselves. What about other sources of joy? Is there a joyous condition that supports flow? Michael Jordan, the Hall of Fame basketball player who spent most of his career with the Chicago Bulls, may be a good example of this. During his professional career, he scored more than forty points in 172 games! And what was one of his most memorable moves? He stuck his tongue out when he was "in the zone," as sports enthusiasts refer to flow. It may have indicated being in a relaxed, even joyful state as he cruised past his defenders, tallying up points. When we know that we are *on fire,* we can relax and enjoy the ride as we burn up the competition.

Phil Jackson was Jordan's coach when the Bulls won three consecutive championships. He was well known for encouraging his athletes to meditate, bringing in George Mumford, a sports psychologist and meditation teacher, to Chicago to train his players. A few years later, Jackson had Mumford train Kobe Bryant and the Los Angeles Lakers. Soon thereafter, the Lakers also won three championships in a row. Pregame meditation sessions were aimed at helping the players relax and let go of hopes of winning, or fears of losing, and to instead focus on the conditions of the moment. Jackson wrote in his book *Eleven Rings: The Soul of Success:* "The most we can hope for is to create the best possible conditions for success, then let go of the outcome. The ride is a lot more fun that way."[5]

The Secret Sauce

In the Pali Canon, joy is described as an explicit condition for concentration during meditation. As noted in chapter 7, it is the fourth factor of awakening leading to tranquility, which then sets up the conditions for concentration. Like curiosity, it has an expansive rather than a contracted quality to it. On the "anger" retreat described in chapter 8, I was practicing setting up the conditions for one-pointed concentration. For this type of meditation, the "recipe" that I had learned included five "ingredients." According to the cookbook, mix the following together and concentration will arise:

Bringing the mind to the object (arousing, applying)
Keeping the mind with the object (sustaining, stretching)
Finding, having interest in the object (joy)
Being happy and content with the object (happiness)
Unifying the mind with the object (fixing)[6]

I repeatedly brought these conditions together and developed longer and longer periods of one-pointedness during the retreat. My concentration kept rising. In one instance, however, I thought that I had brought everything together, yet something was missing. The concentration state wouldn't arise. I sat there puzzled. These steps had worked before. What ingredient was I missing? Then I checked in with my state of mind and realized that I wasn't joyful. That seemed funny to me, and the resultant internal chuckle in my mind was enough to pop me right into the meditative state again. All the other ingredients were already mixed together, waiting for the final one. It simply needed to be added.

Use the Force

As I had done while mountain biking or meditating on retreat, being able to repeatedly reproduce conditions that led to concentration focused in the present moment, the absence of self-evaluation, and an intrinsically joyful experience supported Csíkszentmihályi's assertion that meditation can be a way to get into a flow state. In *Finding Flow: The Psychology of Engagement with Everyday Life* he writes: "In principle any skill or discipline one can master on one's own will serve: meditation and prayer if one is so inclined." Yet as part of establishing the conditions for flow, he emphasized one's attitude or motivation for partaking in the activity: "The important thing, however, is the attitude toward these disciplines. If one prays in order to be holy, or exercises to develop strong pectoral muscles, or learns to be knowledgeable, then a great deal of the benefit is lost. The important thing is to enjoy the activity for its own sake, and to know that what matters is not the result, but the control one is acquiring over one's attention."[7]

One way of interpreting Csíkszentmihályi's focus on attitude is how it affects the elements of flow. For example, if we meditate in order to reach some fantastic state or to "be holy," there is an implicit self-reference in the equation. As the self contracts or grabs onto an experience, "we" become separated from "our" experience. The two can't be merged at that point. In other words, "I" am riding "my" bike. I can't describe some self-transcendent experience unfolding in the now because I am not in it. In other words, the more we work to achieve flow, the more the contraction of excitement may be holding us back from reaching it. Our "me" is in the way.

Another way to look at attitude and its effects on flow is to see how it might engender worry or self-doubt. If we worry that we might crash on a mountain bike descent, the more likely we are to crash. In the movie *Star Wars: The Empire Strikes Back,* Yoda points this out to Luke during his Jedi knight training. Luke has crashed his X-wing fighter into a swamp. As part of his training, he tries to use the "force" to lift it out. Luke works harder and harder, yet the more he tries to lift the fighter, the deeper it sinks. As Luke whines to Yoda that he can't do it, Yoda suggests an alternative to using brute effort.

YODA: "You must unlearn what you have learned."
LUKE: "All right, I'll give it a try"
YODA: "No! Try not! Do, or do not. There is no try."

Yoda is pointing out that self-defeating attitudes such as worry or doubt can get in the way—they are still self-referential, after all. If we stop wondering or worrying whether we can do a task, as long as it is within our skill set, it gets done. The self is optional.

Some biological data back up this idea. During our real-time fMRI neurofeedback study, one of our experienced meditators reported spontaneously dropping into a flow state. After one of her runs, she said, "There was a sense of flow, being with the breath . . . Flow deepened in the middle." The corresponding activity in her PCC, the region of the default mode network most linked with the grab of self, showed a corresponding and notable drop in activity. We had caught flow on film!

Although this is anecdotal evidence, and by no means definitive, it is a nice demonstration linking PCC deactivation to flow. Other brain regions and networks are likely involved in flow—we just don't

An experienced meditator getting into flow during an fMRI scan. The graph shows a significant decrease in PCC activity corresponding to her subjective report of getting into flow (middle of graph). Each bar indicates a two-second measurement. Laboratory archives of Judson Brewer.

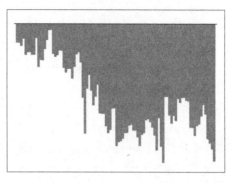

have a good idea (yet) of what they are. Though other brain regions have been investigated in conditions that support flow, such as jazz improvisation and freestyle rap, the PCC is thus far the only area that has been consistently linked with flow.[8] Given the centrality of the lack of self in flow, the PCC may be a marker of one of the necessary conditions for flow to arise.

Musical Flow

Playing music can be one of the best experiences for creating flow, whether performing in a small string or jazz ensemble or large orchestra. Looking back, I had probably been getting into flow as early as high school while playing in a quartet. In college, the entire Princeton Orchestra had a transcendent experience onstage. While on tour in England, we were playing the second movement of Rachmaninoff's Second symphony at the Royal Academy of Music. A little way into it, everything and everyone merged. Time stopped, yet we kept moving. As T. S. Eliot wrote in his magnum opus poem, *Four Quartets:*

At the still point of the turning world. Neither flesh nor flesh-
less;
Neither from nor towards; at the still point, there the
dance is,
But neither arrest nor movement. And do not call it
fixity,
Where past and future are gathered. Neither movement
from nor towards,
Neither ascent nor decline. Except for the point, the still
point,
There would be no dance, and there is only the dance.
I can only say, *there* we have been: but I cannot say
where.
And I cannot say, how long, for that is to place it in time.[9]

After the concert was over, we all pointed to that movement. Something magical had happened. It may have been a perfect confluence of long practice and unity of purpose culminating in a performance in a famous concert hall. Who knows? Regardless, for the next few days, everyone in the orchestra seemed to be glowing.

During my medical and graduate school years, I continued to delight in "the elusive experience of performing enjoyable acts," as Csíkszentmihályi put it, by playing in a semiprofessional quartet. Named the Forza Quartet—after the Italian word for "go!"—we were all musicians who didn't rely on music to pay the bills. We loved to practice and perform just for the sake of playing.

Learning the skills—in this case, practicing music to the point of proficiency—is important for flow to arise. You have to learn the piece. And how we practice may be critical to learning. To give an extreme example: if I lackadaisically practice scales on my violin, even

playing some notes out of tune, doing so will be worse than not practicing at all. Why? Because I will be learning to play out of tune. Just
like bringing together the right ingredients for meditation or a cake
recipe, the quality of musical practice makes a big difference in
whether we will get into flow when performing. If the quality of the
practice is good, the odds that the results will be good increase
dramatically. In a paper entitled "The Psychological Benefits from
Reconceptualizing Music Making as Mindfulness Practice," my
colleague Matt Steinfeld (who trained at Juilliard before becoming a
psychologist and meditator) and I described some of these conditions.[10] The following are a few of the highlights as they relate to flow
and reward-based learning, which can be applied beyond music to
anything we are learning:

☐ Don't beat yourself up. Not surprisingly, as any musician can
   attest, we can become our own worst enemies: berating ourselves
   when rehearsing, getting performance anxiety, or beating
   ourselves up for flubbing a performance. The more we fall
   into these habit loops, the more we practice failure instead of
   success.

☐ Take it slow. Focusing and carefully learning how to play new
   pieces from the beginning can feel tedious at first, yet we must
   make sure to learn the proper technique and mechanics of the
   music. Rushing to play an entire movement of a piece without first
   mastering all its parts can be a sign of restlessness or laziness.

☐ Don't take it personally when you mess up. Learning to drop the
   errors as soon as they come up helps us not compound them.
   Analyzing what we did or wondering whether anyone noticed are
   forms of self-consciousness. Ignoring such potential distractions
   prevents a slipup from becoming a major trip up (or worse).

☐ Quality over quantity. Learning to stop when we are tired or not focused is key. Our ego often says to keep going so that we can boast to ourselves and our fellow musicians that we practiced six hours that day. This suggestion likewise applies to not feeling guilty if we are "supposed" to practice a certain number of hours.

If we practice without paying attention, bad habits slip in more easily. As the famous football coach Vince Lombardi said, "Practice doesn't make perfect. *Perfect* practice makes perfect." The nice thing about music is that it adds a magical ingredient that helps us transcend everyday experience centered on ourselves. When we play music for music's sake, the elements can come together to the point that the music starts singing an uplifting, joyful "hallelujah" unto itself. Perfect practice sets us up to flow.

Dean Potter seems to have lived a happy, though foreshortened, life. He found conditions that he could reproduce to get into a flow state—yet ultimately at a large price. Potter was described in *The Rise of Superman* as preferring flying to sitting in meditation, as favoring "cheating the process" to find flow. "I take the easy way," he said, "I can sit on my ass for two hours to get a fifteen-second glimpse of this state. Or I can risk my life and get there instantly—and it lasts for hours."[11]

Interestingly, over time, I have found the opposite when it comes to meditation. As I have learned to bring the proper ingredients together, my meditation practice has deepened over the years. With it, so has my ability to get into and stay in flow while mountain biking, playing music, and doing other activities. Is it possible that finding the right conditions and practicing them carefully helps our brains reinforce the neural pathways that support flow? It is not surprising that once we identify conditions that trigger intrinsically rewarding behaviors (such as mountain biking, meditation, music, and others), our brains will learn this "behavior," just as it might with anything else. Ironically, instead of getting lulled into mindless habits that leave us disengaged from the world, such as watching television, drinking alcohol, or getting high, we can tap into the same reward-based-learning brain pathways to become more engaged with the world.

10

Training Resilience

When you feel connected to everything, you also feel respon-
sible for everything. And you cannot turn away. Your destiny is
bound with the destinies of others. You must either learn to carry
the Universe or be crushed by it. You must grow strong enough to
love the world, yet empty enough to sit down at the same table with
its worst horrors.

—*Andrew Boyd*

There is a well-known parable of two monks. A wise old monk
quietly hikes along a path with a young novice. They come to a river,
which has a strong, swift current. As the monks prepare to cross, a
young beautiful woman approaches the river and looks at the rushing
water. Fearing that she might get carried away by the current, she asks
whether they can help her get across. The two monks look at each
other; they have taken vows not to touch women. Then, without a
word, the old monk picks up the woman, carries her across, and continues on his journey. The young novice can't believe his eyes. How
could he break monastic code like this? After crossing the river, the
young monk catches up with his companion. He is speechless. His
mind races for hours. Finally, he can't contain himself any longer. He
blurts out, "As monks, we have taken vows not to touch women! How

could you carry that woman on your shoulders?" The wise monk replies, "I set her down on the other side of the river. Why are you still carrying her?"

The elder monk practiced situation-based ethical decision making. His young counterpart could see only that he broke a vow, not that he decreased suffering by coming to the aid of the young woman. The wiser monk attempts to impart the distinction between a helpful guideline and dogma that is too rigid for every circumstance. It is also a beautiful example of what happens when we get in our own way as we continue to hold tight to our views.

This book highlights the idea that if we pay close attention to how our habits are set up, we can break them. Whether mindlessly daydreaming or stealing to buy drugs, each time we get caught up in our behavior, we add weight to the load we carry through our lives. This burden gets compounded when we beat ourselves up for wasting time when we should have been finishing a project, or relapsing again when we know how hard it is on our family members. At times, we can feel like Sisyphus, the king who was punished by the gods to push a boulder up a hill in Hades, only to have it roll back to the bottom, where he had to start pushing it again. He had to repeat this drudgery for eternity. Our lives can feel much the same way: we get nowhere by pushing our own boulders up the hill, and over time, they get pretty heavy. Life doesn't need to be a Sisyphean struggle. We don't need to sweatily shoulder the burden of our habits, pushing the boulder made of them up the mountain again and again. When we become aware of the accumulation of extra baggage, we can begin to shrug it off, unburdening ourselves as we go. Traveling light feels good. As we continue with this process, without the extra weight, our steps get lighter and lighter, and we can eventually slip into flow as our journey unfolds.

Another way to look at the young monk carrying his (optional) burden is through the lens of resilience. Resilience can be defined as follows:

☐ The ability of a substance or object to spring back into shape; elasticity
☐ The capacity to recover quickly from difficulties; toughness

As the story of the monks shows, the younger one was deficient in elasticity. For in fact there is no simple list of rules to be followed in the pursuit of happiness (or holiness). A common formula for happiness is if X, then Y. But that type of happiness is dependent upon something external to ourselves, and doesn't take into account the fact that we, and our environment, are constantly changing. Many, many times, the "if X, then Y" formula doesn't work or quickly becomes outdated simply because our world has changed. The same is true of the habits that we form as we go through life. In our constant search for stability, we develop habitual if-X-then-Y responses based on external and internal triggers, which also become outdated.

This habituation is often felt as resistance. Lolo, our hurdler, and Dean, our flow enthusiast, began by being flexible enough in their bodies and aimed for the same flexibility in their minds. What happens when this isn't the case, when we do the opposite? How many times have we or a coworker suggested trying something new at work, only to have the proposal set off a wave of resistance before the idea could even be explained or unpacked? We might feel this both physically and mentally as a closing down or a contraction.

I have seen this time and time again with my patients. They walk into my office, and I can immediately tell from the furtive glances or lack of eye contact that something is up. Someone who has been do-ing very well—staying clean or sober for months or longer—launches into a story about how a family member got sick, how she or her spouse lost a job, how her romantic relationship broke down, or how some other major life event upended her recovery. She got caught up in resisting what was happening, not wanting it to be so, which made it harder for her to be present and work with it.

Worse, they tell me how they relapsed because they couldn't han-dle the stress. Without some type of training to increase their pliancy or resilience, the old habits come back with a vengeance—"This is just what I do when things get tough," they tell me. Their prefrontal cortex goes offline from the stress, and they revert to the familiar and automatic habits of smoking, drinking, or using drugs. And by auto-matic, I really mean automatic—they often describe "waking up" in the middle of smoking a cigarette or going on a bender, completely confused about how the half-burnt cigarette got in their mouths. Af-ter they get the story off of their chest, we dive into the details of their relapse. They invariably point out how their relapse not only didn't help anything, but also (surprise) made matters worse. Without that necessary extra little bit of mental flexibility, they defaulted to old habits. It is like a string on an instrument being wound too tight—any additional pressure will break it.

If we can develop a mental pliancy with which to approach the many changes and challenges that arise in life, we can loosen the strings or grease the skids; unnecessary burdens that arise from resist-ing what is happening in any moment will become easier to bear. As a result, we will be able to bounce back from difficulty and be elastic enough to bend as things change. At the far end of the spectrum, events that we view as difficult can be opportunities for growth. The Tao Te Ching states it thus:

The mark of a moderate man
is freedom from his own ideas.
Tolerant like the sky,
all-pervading like sunlight,
firm like a mountain,
supple like a tree in the wind,
he has no destination in view
and makes use of anything
life happens to bring his way.
Nothing is impossible for him
because he has let go.[1]

Let's now look at specific ways in which we habitually harden, and also at how to use those habits as opportunities to build our resilience instead of stumbling over them—how to get our bounce back and become more elastic in the process.

Empathy Fatigue

Let's start with the empathy. Empathy is the "ability to understand and share feelings of another." Being able to put ourselves in the shoes of another is generally thought to be a very helpful tool. At the same time, as we have seen, *how* we relate to our situation—in this case, putting ourselves in someone else's shoes—is every bit as important as the situation itself.

In medical school, we were taught to empathize with our patients. Most doctors (myself among them) and other medical professionals study medicine with the aim of helping others. The emphasis on empathy makes sense: the more that we can walk in our patients' shoes, the more likely it is that we will be able to help them. Studies have shown that higher "empathy scores" in doctors indeed correlate with faster recovery times for their patients, whether they are getting over colds or learning to better control their blood sugar.[2] Unfortunately, empathy has been shown to decrease during the third year of medical school—the time when most medical students are finishing up their coursework and beginning their clinical rotations. That decline continues into new doctors' residencies and beyond. By the time they become practicing physicians, up to 60 percent of physicians report feeling burned out. For example, they report that they start treating their patients like objects, that they feel emotionally exhausted, and so on. They lose their bounce.[3]

We physicians certainly wouldn't be inducted into the resilience hall of fame (or even nominated!). This widespread phenomenon is now described as "empathy fatigue." Many factors likely contribute to this. If we are good at putting ourselves in our patients' shoes, and our patients are suffering, then we are suffering, too. When we wake up to the fact that suffering is painful, we naturally protect ourselves from it. See suffering (trigger), protectively contract or distance ourselves (behavior), feel better (reward). With each contraction, we become more rigid, less resilient.

Herein lies a conundrum. Nobody argues that physicians should be martyrs, throwing themselves under the suffering bus so that they can make sure their patients' blood sugar levels are well controlled. Yet our patients seem to do better when we can relate to them. How do we work with this seeming paradox? The first step is to test our working hypothesis: are we reacting to our patients' suffering in a way that leads us to suffer? Ironically, according to the conventional definition of empathy, if the answer were yes, we would score a perfect ten on the empathy scale. We must be missing something here. Indeed, the definitions of empathy in the medical profession may still be in flux—they should take into account more than just "the ability to understand and share the feelings of another."

What might be missing from the standard definition of empathy is the motivation behind the action. Doctors go into medicine to help people decrease their suffering. Taking this into account, how do we learn to stay connected with our patients without being burnt out by that connection? The idea of compassion comes into play here. The word "compassion" comes from the Latin root *compati*, meaning to "suffer with." (The word "patient" likewise derives from *pati*, "to suffer.") Does practicing compassion help us suffer with someone (that is, "feel their pain") without being sucked into it? The answer may be yes.

To get sucked in, there must be *someone* getting sucked in. As noted throughout this book, there are many ways to perpetuate our sense of self. If we learn not to take things personally—that is, not to view them from a "how is this affecting me?" perspective—many possibilities open up. Framed from a Buddhist perspective, dropping our habitual and subjective reactivity will cause the suffering to drop as well. In his book *The Compassionate Life*, the spiritual leader of Tibet, His Holiness the Dalai Lama wrote: "Compassion without attachment is possible. Therefore, we need to clarify the distinctions between compassion and attachment. True compassion is not just an emotional response but also a firm commitment founded on reason. Because of this firm foundation, a truly compassionate attitude toward others does not change even if they behave negatively. Genuine compassion is based not on our own projections and expectations, but rather on the needs of the other: irrespective of whether another person is a close friend or an enemy . . . This is genuine compassion."[4]

The contraction that puts up a protective barrier so that we don't get hurt feels very different from a response that isn't seeded in self-preservation. If we can clearly see the different types of reactions triggered by bearing witness to suffering, we can differentiate those that are based on reward-based learning (self-protective) from genuine compassion (selfless).

When I am in the face of suffering, it is easy to differentiate a selfish response from a selfless one—the former feels like a closing down, while the latter feels expansive. This expansive quality of experience shares characteristics of loving-kindness and flow—the self-referential, contracted "me" part of my mind is out of the way. Additionally, with "me" on the sidelines (or not even in the stadium), I don't have to worry about protecting myself from getting tackled or injured on the field. Bringing this recognition back to the idea of empathy fatigue: removal of the "me" element frees up the energy devoted to self-protection, obviating the resultant fatigue. In other words, it is exhausting to take my patients' suffering personally. It is freeing if I don't. Our patients can tell the difference in how we walk into their hospital rooms, make eye contact, listen, and answer their questions. This whole realm of communication can come across as clinical, closed, and sterile, or warm and open. The latter experience shows up in patients' increased satisfaction scores and improved health outcomes. And it works both ways.

Mick Krasner and Ron Epstein, physicians at the University of Rochester School of Medicine and Dentistry, were interested in whether mindfulness training could decrease empathy fatigue in physicians.[5] They developed an intensive educational program to develop self-awareness, mindfulness, and communication. They trained primary care physicians over the course of eight weeks and measured burnout and empathy scores (among others) both at the end of the training and a year later.

Compared to baseline, Krasner and colleagues found significant differences in a number of measures, including reduced burnout and increased empathy and emotional stability. Their results provide empirical support for the idea that when we don't get caught up in our own reactions, both we and our patients benefit. As these aspects of physician and patient care become clearer, it will be interesting to see whether the medical definitions of empathy evolve to include a more compassion-based understanding, moving from putting ourselves in someone else's shoes in a way that promotes our own suffering, to walking with someone in the midst of their suffering. Perhaps empathy training will be replaced by compassion training and related techniques. Some medical schools are already incorporating mindfulness into their curricula.

Medical practice is just one of the myriad ways in which we can tune in to our experiences in order to differentiate selfish reactions (biased toward protecting "me") from selfless responses (situation-based and spontaneous), whether in our professional or personal lives.

When I don't take suffering personally, that freed-up energy can get recycled into helping. In fact, when seeing suffering clearly, I feel a natural movement to help. Many of us have had these experiences. Whether a friend calls on the phone in emotional distress, or we see a major natural disaster on the news, when we step back from worrying about ourselves, what happens? Paradoxically, we *lean in,* moving toward the suffering, whether by lending an ear, sending a donation, or otherwise. Why? Who knows for sure? As we know with loving-kindness or generosity, it certainly feels good to help. And by helping us learn to let go of our reactive habits, including self-protection, this type of reward should naturally increase our resilience.

(Un-) Resistance Training

This book has explored many ways in which, through no fault of our own, we orient ourselves toward some type of dis-ease. Whether it is the excitement of getting "likes" on Facebook, the reinforcement of some type of self-view, or simply getting caught up in thought, these self-focused activities have consequences that we can feel physically as clenching, restlessness, or an energetic push to "do something." The more we reinforce any of these habits, the more "grooved" they become in our brain circuitry and corresponding behavior. The deeper we groove these pathways, the more likely they are to become ruts that we get stuck in—or to switch metaphors, they become the kind of worldview glasses worn so naturally that we don't even notice we have them on.

When we run into resistance of some sort, it can be a signal that we are stuck in a rut or a hole—ironically, the one that we have been grooving. As we become entrenched in a view or a behavior, we dig ourselves in deeper and deeper. We have all experienced this sensation during an argument. At some point, we realize that we are just dogmatically duking it out and that our arguments are becoming more and more ridiculous. Yet for some reason, our egos won't let us back down. We have forgotten the "law of holes": when in a hole, stop digging.[6]

In addition, the book has shown how simple mindful awareness can help us see whether we are digging ourselves deeper into that hole (that is, seeing the world through our subjective biases) or reinforcing patterns that are setting us up for more dis-ease in the future. Dis-ease or stress can be our compass—when we orient based on it. Mindfulness helps us look at our compass so that we can see whether we are moving toward or away from suffering, digging a deeper hole or putting the shovel down. Let's unpack this idea a bit more.

What does it take to make a compass? Because the earth has north and south magnetic poles, a freely moving ferromagnetic needle will line up, or orient itself, with its ends pointing north and south. In other words, given certain causes or conditions (the earth has magnetic poles, and the needle is magnetic), we can expect or predict specific effects or results (the needle will orient in a certain direction). Once the earth's magnetic fields were discovered, people could make compasses that worked all over the world. If I knew these basic principles, I could teach you how to make a compass; no special needles or ceremonies are required—just the right materials. With this knowledge, I could also predict the circumstances when the compass won't work, for example, when it is in the vicinity of a magnet.

As mentioned earlier, the origins of mindfulness date back 2,500 years to the Indian subcontinent and a historical figure named Siddhartha Gautama (aka the Buddha), who lived roughly from 563 to 483 BCE. Interestingly, some of his simplest and most famous teachings sound like physics explanations of why compasses work. He asserted that human behavior could be described in terms of conditionality: much of it follows straightforward rules, similar to natural laws (such as "a compass points north and south"). Based on these rules, he went on, we can predict that particular causes will lead to particular outcomes.

The Buddha focused his teachings exclusively on suffering: "I teach one thing and one thing only: suffering [dis-ease, stress] and the end of suffering." It is important to point out this core principle, since it was the compass by which he oriented his teachings. Having supposedly figured out the human psychology governing dis-ease, he could teach those natural laws to others so that they could learn to see clearly the causes of dis-ease and, by extension, ways to end it.

The title of the first teaching of the Pali Canon has been translated as "setting in motion the wheel of truth."[7] In it, the Buddha describes perhaps the best-known aspects of Buddhism in pop culture: the four noble truths. He begins by opening the compass and showing us where dis-ease comes from: "The Noble Truth of Suffering (*dukkha*), monks, is this: . . . association with the unpleasant is suffering, dissociation from the pleasant is suffering, not receiving what one desires is suffering." He shows that there is a logical nature to our actions, which is as straightforward as a compass lining up according to the laws of physics. When someone yells at us, it doesn't feel good. Nor does it when we are separated from our loved ones. And just as a compass continually orients to north and south, repeating these actions generally brings about the same results.

Next, having pointed out the logical nature of dis-ease, he lays out its cause. He states: "The Noble Truth of the Origin [cause] of Suffering is this: It is this craving." When someone yells at us, he suggests that *wanting* that person to stop yelling makes things worse. Similarly, pining and whining when our spouse or partner is away on a trip doesn't magically make her (let's say) appear in our arms (and certainly annoys our friends). This teaching is analogous to a physics professor painting a red mark on a compass and saying, "That is north." Previously, we knew only that one of the directions led toward suffering; now we are oriented to north and south. If we walk south (cause), we will suffer (effect). We can start using stress as a compass simply by looking at it.

The Buddha then makes a third statement: "Giving [craving] up, relinquishing it, liberating oneself from it" results in "the complete cessation of that very craving." Walk north, and your suffering will diminish. If our sweetheart is away for a week, see what happens if we stop daydreaming about her and focus on what is in front of us (we might feel better). If we are deeply engaged in the task at hand, we might forget about the hours left until she returns—and then *bam!* she is back.

Finally, the Buddha lays out a path to the fourth truth, which leads "to the cessation of suffering." He provides a detailed map.

In *After Buddhism,* Stephen Batchelor describes these four noble truths as a "fourfold task":

> to comprehend suffering,
> to let go of the arising of reactivity,
> to behold the ceasing of reactivity, and
> to cultivate a . . . path that is grounded in the perspective of
> *mindful awareness*[8]

Framed in this way, the language of the Buddha's first teaching (pleasant, unpleasant, suffering) and his emphasis on cause and effect sound like operant conditioning. Acting in an automatic or knee-jerk manner to quickly satisfy a craving just feeds it. We have looked at many examples of this habit loop. In life, we habitually react to our circumstances based on our subjective biases, especially when we don't get what we want. Dropping into a mindful awareness of our habitual reactivity helps us step out of the cycle of suffering—resting in awareness itself rather than being caught up in reactivity. Batchelor lays this out in no uncertain terms: "'The arising' denotes craving; greed, hatred, and delusion . . . that is, whatever reactivity is triggered by our contact with the world. "'The ceasing' denotes the ending of that reactivity."[9]

Returning to the idea of resilience, we can see how reactivity amounts to the opposite of resilience: resistance. Why do we resist a new idea without thinking it through? We are reacting according to some type of subjective bias. Why do we resist getting dumped by our sweetheart, sometimes with begging and pleading? We are reacting to that ego blow or potential loss of security. When we are resilient, we can bend with new circumstances as we begin to experience them. When we are resilient, we don't resist or avoid the grieving process.

We recover faster without our ego attachment and feeling of threat; we move on without holding on.

As we go through the day, seeing how many times we react to or resist things beyond our control can help us see more clearly that we are training our own resistance. We are building up our muscles to be able to fight that "bad" (new) idea. We are building our defenses to fend off that hurt when we get dumped. The extreme end of this spectrum is to steel ourselves, to not allow ourselves to be open and vulnerable. In their song "I Am a Rock," Paul Simon and Art Garfunkel describe building walls of protection so that "no one touches me," an ill-fated attempt to avoid the emotional roller coaster of life. Isolation as the solution to suffering: an island never cries.

As the folk rock duo point out, resistance has a price. The more we wall ourselves off from the world, the more we miss. Remember our logic-based System 2, our self-control mechanism? Mr. Spock has no emotions. He is optimized for unbiased action. For most humans, emotions (domain of the usually dominant System 1) go to the core of who we are, so System 2 doesn't work very well when we get stressed or otherwise overly emotional.

In any type of addictive behavior, reactivity builds its strength through repetition—resistance training. Each time we look for our "likes" on Facebook, we lift the barbell of "I am." Each time we smoke a cigarette in reaction to a trigger, we do a push-up of "I smoke." Each time we excitedly run off to a colleague to tell her about our latest and greatest idea, we do a sit-up of "I'm smart." That is a lot of work.

At some point we stop running around in the circles perpetuating our (perpetual) positive and negative reinforcement loops. When does this happen? Usually when we are exhausted—once we have grown tired of all the lever pressing and start to wake up to the fact that it isn't getting us anywhere. When we stop and look at our own life, we can step back and see that we are lost, headed nowhere. We can pull out our compass and see that we have been orienting ourselves in the wrong direction. The beautiful thing here is that *simply by paying attention* to how we are causing our own stress—simply by being mindful—we can begin to train ourselves to walk the other way.

Our resistance training will not have been in vain, though. It will help remind us of the behaviors that move us in the wrong direction—toward increased dis-ease and dissatisfaction. The more clearly we see this unwanted result arising from a repeated behavior, the more disenchanted we become, and the less we will be *naturally* drawn to move toward that behavior. The excitement that was formerly a supposed source of happiness no longer does it for us. Why? Because the reward of letting go and simply being feels better than dis-ease. Our brains are set up to learn. As soon as we clearly see the difference between a contracted, self-reinforcing reward and an open, expanding, joyful self-forgetting one, we will have learned to read the compass. We can then orient ourselves and begin moving in the other direction—toward true happiness. Knowing how an instrument works is tremendously empowering; we can use it to its fullest extent. With our own suffering, instead of shrinking away from it or beating ourselves up for having gotten caught up in yet another habit loop, we can pull out our compass and ask ourselves, "Where am I headed with this?" We can even bow to our habit in a gesture of gratitude because in fact, in this moment, it is acting as a teacher, helping us learn about ourselves and our habitual reactivity so that we can grow from the experience.

Let's continue with the resistance-training metaphor. When training in a gym, we calculate how much to lift, how many times to lift it, and how long to hold it against gravity (resistance). Each aspect of the exercise contributes to the strengthening of our muscles. The young monk in the parable at the beginning of the chapter lifted his mental burden once, yet kept holding it up until it became too heavy. When he couldn't take it anymore, he angrily threw it down at the feet of his colleague.

When starting any type of un- or antiresistance training, whether taking a Mindfulness-Based Stress Reduction course or using some other way to change, we can apply these three types of gym metrics to our reactivity as we go about our day. *How often* do we react by taking something personally? The simplest way to find out is to look for some type of internal contraction denoting an urge or attachment— remember, this physical sensation occurs with both pleasant and unpleasant experiences. *How heavy* is the burden, meaning, how contracted do we get? And finally, *how long* do we carry it around? Gaining a clear view of our reactivity will naturally point us to its opposite: letting go. We can use the same metrics to check our progress in this area. How often do we let go or not habitually react in a way that we used to? When we pick something up, is it lighter than before, meaning, do we not get as caught up in it? How long do we carry it around? And if we notice that we have been carrying something around, how quickly do we drop it (and not pick it back up)?

We can think of antiresistance training as an exploration more than a dogmatic framework for achieving some result. Orienting to stress and its opposite doesn't lead us to *something in particular.* Instead, paying attention helps us start moving in a *particular direction, at any moment.* The more we become familiar with our compass, the easier it becomes to realize how readily available this mode of being is, all the time. We don't have to do anything special or go somewhere to get something. We simply have to learn what it feels like to get in our own way, and the rest begins to take care of itself. Keeping our eyes open, seeing clearly, will keep us moving in that direction.

T. S. Eliot wrote at the end of the fourth of the *Four Quartets:*

We shall not cease from exploration
And the end of all our exploring
Will be to arrive where we started
And know the place for the first time.
Through the unknown, remembered gate
When the last of earth left to discover
Is that which was the beginning;

What are we looking for? He tells us a few lines later:

Not known, because not looked for
But heard, half-heard, in the stillness
Between two waves of the sea.
Quick now, here, now, always—
A condition of complete simplicity
(Costing not less than everything)

Within the context of this book, the "everything" that he refers to can be interpreted as every set of glasses that we have put on during our lives and continue to wear as we build up, defend, and protect our sense of self. What happens when we shed all these subjective biases, let go of our own worldview, and completely get out of our own way? He finishes:

And all shall be well and
All manner of thing shall be well

When the tongues of flame are in-folded
Into the crowned knot of fire
And the fire and the rose are one.[10]

Sounds pretty rewarding.

Epilogue: The Future Is Now

You can't enforce happiness. You can't in the long run enforce anything. We don't use force! All we need is adequate behavioral engineering.

—*Mr. Frazier, in* Walden Two, *by B. F. Skinner*

We have explored throughout this book how it is possible to get addicted to almost anything: cigarettes, alcohol, narcotics, and even self-images. It isn't our fault. It is in our DNA to pair action with outcome, stimulus with reward, in order to survive. Studies of behavior by Skinner and others have shown that understanding how these learning processes work can help us change them for the better.

Seeing broader implications of this discovery, Skinner took the notion a step further, suggesting that this learning process can apply to everything, including sex and politics. *Walden Two* (1948), his only novel, is set just after World War II somewhere in America's heartland. It describes an intentional, utopian society—a natural progression and societal extension of his work with animals. In *Walden Two*, Skinner emphasizes the engineering of self-control as a way to achieve this ideal, which, while a noble idea, may have some inherent limitations given our current state of brain evolution.

Interestingly, the Buddhist psychologists may have stumbled on a solution when they examined the same processes as Skinner. Focusing on the self and the development of subjective biases through reward-based learning as the core of the afflictive process, they may have identified not only a key component (craving and reactivity) of the process, but an elegantly simple solution as well: paying attention to the perceived rewards of our actions. Seeing the outcomes of actions more clearly helps us reduce our subjective biases, and this reorientation naturally leads to our stepping out of unhealthy habits, moving from stress toward a type of happiness that isn't dependent upon our getting something. Making this adjustment frees up vital energy, which can be redirected toward improving our lives, whether that means being less distracted, engaging with the world more fully, finding greater happiness, and even experiencing flow. If any of this is true (and mounting scientific evidence continues to point in this direction), what is getting in the way?

Mad Scientists

In *Walden Two,* Skinner makes several references to the fact that the world outside the intentional community already deploys behavioral engineering in everyday life. Billboards are big and enticing; nightclubs and other types of entertainment get people excited so they will pay money to see the show. He highlights the rampant use of propaganda and other tactics used to corral the masses through fear and excitement. Of course, these are examples of positive and negative reinforcement. When a certain tactic works, it is more likely to be repeated. For example, you don't need to look further than any recent election to see how a politician may run on a platform of fear (behavior): "The country is not safe! I will make it safe!" The thought of being harmed urges the electorate to support that person. If the strategy works to get that person elected (reward), we can bet that similar ones will be used in the next election, given supportive conditions (there has to be a "credible" threat).

This type of behavioral engineering may seem somewhat banal or benign, partially because of its ubiquity and time scale. After all, presidential elections occur only every four years, and fear-based election campaigns are not new. Yet advancements in our scientific understanding of psychology and reward-based learning can be coupled with modern technology to essentially pull off what Skinner was worried about—on an unprecedented level. One of his emphases in *Walden Two* was the ability of certain organizations to perform science experiments on an entire community, giving them unambiguous results relatively quickly. The size of Walden Two was 1,000 people. A modern multinational company might have *billions* of customers who use its products daily. The company's engineers can selectively tweak this or that product component and have conclusive results within days or even hours, depending on how many people they include in their experiment.

Social scientists have found that positive and negative emotions can be transferred from one person to others nearby (this phenomenon is known as emotional contagion). If someone in an obviously happy mood walks into a room, others are more likely to likewise feel happy, as if the emotion were contagious. In a collaboration with Cornell University, Facebook's Adam Kramer wanted to see whether this phenomenon could be true in digital interactions—in a social network.[1] The newsfeed data from 700,000 Facebook users was manipulated to change the amount of emotional content that users would see (positive and negative separately). When the researchers reduced the number of posts with positive expressions, users followed suit: they produced fewer positive posts. A mixed effect occurred with negative expressions: as they were reduced, users posted less negative *and* more positive content. This type of "behavioral engineering" was exactly what Skinner had predicted—seventy years ago!

This study became controversial, partly because of concerns about the ethics of (not) obtaining participants' consent. It was unclear whether users had adequately "signed up" for the study by agreeing to Facebook's terms of use. Typically, participants are informed about what they are getting into; if deception is part of the experiment, an ethics board has to agree that the benefits of the deception outweigh the risks. Interestingly, one of the reasons why the controversy came to light was that the study was published. When a company isn't dependent on scientific publications to generate revenue, it can do unlimited experimentation in the name of customer acquisition and revenue generation, behind closed doors.

Given currently available technology, a company of virtually any size can do what is known as A/B testing, in which a single variable is manipulated and its effect on an outcome is noted. The larger the sample, the more definitive the results. Large companies with sizable customer bases and resources can engineer our behavior relatively rapidly and more or less continually.

Behavioral engineering happens in every industry in which Skinnerian techniques can be employed. Why wouldn't they be? If we are trying to get people to buy our stuff, we need to figure out what motivates them to move (their "pain point"). Another example is food engineering. In 2013, Michael Moss published "The Extraordinary Science of Addictive Junk Food," a revealing article about the food industry, in the *New York Times Magazine*.[2] He described all the ways that food is manipulated to perfect its color, smell, taste, and feel. Food can be engineered to activate our dopamine systems so that we will eat more, even when we aren't hungry. Remember: this is where the whole evolutionary story started. We have to eat to survive. When mouth-watering food is plentiful, we learn to gobble it up when we are happy, sad, anxious, restless, or bored. The unfortunate reality is that this kind of engineering is being used to keep us overconsuming, whether the reward is food, drugs, social media, or shopping.

I am not pointing out this ubiquitous feature of contemporary life in order to scare people. These are long-standing practices that will gain momentum as markets expand and we become more globally interconnected. Besides, as Skinner pointed out, fear can be used to manipulate, too. As a psychiatrist, friend, husband, teacher, and brother, I have seen so much suffering that *my* pain point has been reached—it hurts to suffer and to see others suffering. Feeling this pain, I became motivated to do something to help. And so I am using what I have learned about the causes of suffering to help educate people so that they can develop their own tools to decrease it—both for themselves and for others.

If You Can't Beat 'Em, Join 'Em

Jeff Walker is a towering yet soft-spoken old-school gentleman who was introduced to me by a friend because he wanted to see what my lab's real-time fMRI neurofeedback was all about. After retiring early from the private equity industry in 2007, Walker increasingly spent his time helping nonprofit enterprises raise money. He had found working with boards and leaders in the nonprofit sector to be rewarding, even going as far as writing a book called *The Generosity Network.*

Given our many shared interests (including music and meditation), I agreed to give Jeff a spin in our fMRI machine. Once in the scanner, we had him try different meditation techniques, improvisation of music, and so on while he watched his posterior cingulate cortex activity go up and down. After about an hour and a half, seemingly satisfied with what he had seen, he climbed out of the machine and took me to lunch. Once we sat down with our food, he told me that I was going to start a company, and he sketched it out on a napkin. "These tools need to make it out into the world," he said between bites of his sandwich.

Forming a company was the last thing I had in mind. I was (and am) a scientist—I went to graduate school to find truth and to understand how the world works. I was a bit anxious, but Jeff convinced me that the company would be a good way to help people and to move our work beyond the ivory tower of academia. We set up the company with the backing of some like-minded angel investors who were focused on social change rather than return on investment. We first called the company goBlue Labs because Yale's colors are blue and white, and the neurofeedback graph would show up as blue when someone was deactivating his or her PCC. We then changed it to Claritas MindSciences, since *claritas* is Latin for "clarity" or "brightness," and the idea was that simply by seeing clearly, we can overcome addictive behavior.

The aim of the start-up was to bring to the public what we had learned in the lab about reward-based learning—and thereby challenge the consumerism stream by teaching people to reorient their compasses. As with some of the novices (in chapter 4) who tapped into the experience of "letting go," perhaps we could develop devices and training programs that would help people do this deliberately. We sincerely believed that it was time to put to work the knowledge that my lab had garnered, given the rise in addictions that are reinforced by the conditions in our world today.

Ironically, Kathy Carroll and her research team at Yale had been studying how best to disseminate behavioral therapies so that they would maintain their potency and efficacy. Led by Steve Martino, Carroll's group had recently published a paper showing that trained therapists who knew that they were being tape-recorded for a study still spent a large amount of time in their sessions in "informal discussion" with their clients—in other words, chatting. A whopping 88 percent of them spent some part of the session *initiating* discussions about *themselves*.[3] Brain "rewards" aside, such unnecessary conversations weren't helping their patients. With this fact in hand, Carroll had developed a computerized delivery of cognitive behavioral therapy in which videotaped instruction and role-playing replaced one-on-one counseling. The results showed it to be effective for substance use treatment.[4]

Following Carroll's lead, our start-up took digital therapeutic delivery a step further. We reasoned that if people had developed habits in particular contexts (for example, learning to smoke in their cars) and were already addicted to their phones, perhaps we could use the same technology that was driving them to distraction to help them step out of their unhealthy habit patterns of smoking, stress eating, and other addictive behaviors. We need to engage with our inherent capacity to be curiously aware when the urge to smoke, eat out of stress, or engage in some other compulsive behavior is triggered.

To that end, we digitized our manualized mindfulness training so that it can be delivered via smartphone (or the Web) in bite-size pieces. As the tagline goes, "Yes, we have an app for that." Using specific pain points related to smoking ("Craving to Quit") and stress eating ("Eat Right Now"), our first two programs provide daily training that consists of videos, animations, and in-the-moment exercises introducing people to mindfulness training in short daily segments (usually no more than five to ten minutes of training a day). We have paired the training with online communities that only people in the program can join; they are encouraged to support one another as peers. I can join in to give practice tips and suggestions. And we can study the apps in clinical trials to see how well they work.

In May 2013, about a year after our start-up was launched, I was in the Washington, DC, area. I had just finished consulting on a meditation research study at Johns Hopkins University for a couple of days and filming a TEDx talk on mindfulness. Being in the area, I made an appointment to meet with Tim Ryan, a congressman from Ohio. Tim and I had met at a party at a contemplative science research conference the previous year. He had been blown away after attending his first meditation retreat a few years before with Jon Kabat-Zinn, and had started meditating daily. Seeing how mindfulness could help ease partisanship in Congress, he started a weekly meditation group in the House of Representatives, and in 2012 published a book entitled *A Mindful Nation: How a Simple Practice Can Help Us Reduce Stress, Improve Performance, and Recapture the American Spirit.*

At his office, Tim jumped right in and asked for an update on the latest mindfulness research. He impressed me by really trying to understand the facts and science behind something before supporting it. As we talked, I mentioned our recent findings on mindfulness and smoking cessation, and our recent development of an app to deliver the training digitally. As I started showing him the program's features on my phone, he jumped up and called to one of his young staff members, "Hey Michael, come in here!" "You smoke, don't you?" asked Tim as Michael came into the room. He sheepishly said yes. "Well, you don't have to quit, but try this app out and tell me if it's any good," Tim said. Michael nodded and left the room.

On the train ride north that afternoon, I sent Michael an e-mail: "Thanks for volunteering (or being volunteered by Congressman Ryan) to help test out our Craving to Quit program," and then I gave him the details on how to get started. Two days later he started the program. The following week, he e-mailed me about his progress, ending with: "Thank you again [for] giving me this opportunity, I was not planning on quitting, but now that I am doing the program I figure now is as good a time as any." I received a follow-up e-mail from Michael a month later: "I began this program a skeptic, but saw its benefits almost immediately. I went from smoking 10 cigarettes a day, literally afraid to leave the house without a pack and a lighter, and after 21 days I have been able to stop smoking all together, this would have never been possible without Craving to Quit." As I read this, tears streamed down my face. My wife asked what happened, and I stammered, "This may actually work."

Over a year later, Anderson Cooper was visiting my lab at the Center for Mindfulness to film a story for CBS's *60 Minutes*. He had just come from interviewing Congressman Ryan. I asked Denise, the show's producer, about Michael. Yes, she remembered him—and mentioned that he told her he was still smoke-free.

Craving to Quit is now in clinical trials comparing it to active control conditions that my lab set up, and in head-to-head comparison studies with smoking-cessation apps developed by the National Cancer Institute. We have made it publicly available, too, so that we can get feedback from smokers around the world on how it works for them—and so that we can continually improve the program. We have also launched a related program to help individuals overcome stress and emotional eating: Eat Right Now (as in, eat correctly, in the present moment). One of the nice features of these programs, especially the online communities, is that our users, in addition to supporting one another (giving is rewarding!), are building a crowd-sourced knowledge base for these practices. Each time someone keeps a journal of his or her progress, or I answer a question, it adds to the project. Future users will be able to benefit from this accumulated knowledge and experience—a tangible example of "pay it forward."

We are working on other tools for the digital delivery of mindfulness. Since we know that reward-based learning works best via feedback (reward), Claritas and my lab have been working together closely to develop neurofeedback tools that don't require a multimillion-dollar fMRI machine. Prasanta (the physicist whom I introduced in chapter 3), Dr. Remko van Lutterveld (a senior postdoctoral fellow in the lab), and the rest of our team are developing an EEG device that does almost the same thing as our fMRI neurofeedback—records changes in the PCC related to getting caught up in our experience, and to letting go. The best types of feedback are ones from which we learn something no matter whether the signal is increased or decreased, and in pilot testing, we are finding that our device informs individuals' experience in the same way—it is helpful to know what both types of experiences feel like so that the former behavior can be abandoned, and the latter supported.

Eventually, we aim to bring together neurofeedback and app-based training programs in a way that will help people change habits using evidence-based training that is standardized yet personalized—providing mindfulness tools and the feedback necessary to ensure that the tools are being used properly.

In a world that is swimming closer and closer to a vortex of short-term rewards that leave us thirsty for more, might these types of tools, by tapping into the same types of reinforcement processes, give us the opportunity to discover how much of a good thing is enough, whether it is food, money, prestige, or power? Through such a journey of discovery, we may uncover more lasting and satisfying rewards. And by learning mindfulness, we may learn to live with more awareness and care, consciously deciding whether to engage in all kinds of behaviors rather than mindlessly pressing levers for dopamine spritzes. We might discover a happier, healthier life rather than one that is just more full of shallow excitement.

What Is Your Mindfulness Personality Type?

In chapter 3, we discussed extreme personality dysfunction in relation to reward-based learning. In this way, we could get a handle on how personality is set up more broadly. Throughout the book, we explored specific examples of behaviors that, with repetition, become habits and even addictions.

If these extremes of behavior are reinforced by associative learning, what about everyday, run-of-the-mill behavior? Could much of our behavior be attributed to "approach and avoid": approaching that which we find attractive or pleasant, and avoiding that which we find repulsive or unpleasant? Could this even explain our (nonpathological) personalities?

Our research team recently found that a fifth-century Buddhist "meditation manual," entitled the *Path of Purification,* describes how quite a few, perhaps all, personality traits fall into one of three buckets: faithful/greedy, discerning/aversive, and speculative/deluded.[1] The manual describes everyday characteristics, such as the type of food one eats, how one walks or dresses, and so forth, as ways to measure or determine which bucket someone generally falls into:

By the posture, by the action,
By eating, seeing, and so on,

By the kind of states occurring,
May temperament be recognized.

For example, when walking into a party, someone of the faithful/ greedy type might look around and marvel at the wonderful food that is being served, and excitedly start mingling with friends that she sees. In contrast, a discerning/aversive type might notice how the furniture didn't quite match, and later in the night be found arguing with someone over the accuracy of her statement. The speculative/deluded type would be more likely to go with the flow.

Why did the writers of this manual bother compiling this typology? So they could give personalized recommendations for people who were learning to meditate. The manual may be one of the first guides to what we now think of as personalized medicine—matching a treatment to an individual's phenotype.

Our research group recently took this classification scheme one step further: we found that the behavioral tendencies line up with modern mechanisms of associative learning—approach, avoid, freeze. We tested forty-three questions with roughly 900 volunteers, and from their data we developed and validated a thirteen-question "behavioral tendencies questionnaire (BTQ)" that anyone can take.[2] The BTQ is now being studied as a tool for predicting and personalizing modern mindfulness and lifestyle practices.

By more clearly seeing and understanding our tendencies in everyday life, we can learn about ourselves and our habitual responses to our internal and external worlds. We can learn the personality types of family members, friends, and coworkers, which might allow us to live and work together more harmoniously. For example, a predominantly faithful/greedy type might do well in marketing or sales. One might give a discerning/aversive type a project that needs a high level of precision and attention to detail. And a speculative/deluded type might be the best at coming up with creative ideas during a brainstorming session.

We have listed the questions below so you can get a general sense of what category or categories you fall into. The actual scoring is a bit trickier—to get accurate percentages, you can take the quiz on the UMass Center for Mindfulness's website.

Behavioral Tendencies Questionnaire (Short Form)

Please rank the following in the order that is most consistent with how you generally behave (not how you think you should behave, or how you might behave in a very specific situation). You should give your first and initial response without thinking about the question too much. Place a 1 by the answer that best fits you, followed by a 2 for your second choice, and a 3 for the answer that least fits you.

1. If I were to plan a party, . . .

   _____ A. I would want it to be high energy, with lots of people.
   _____ B. I would only want certain people there.
   _____ C. it would be last minute and freeform.

2. When it comes to cleaning my room, I . . .

   _____ A. take pride in making things look great.
   _____ B. quickly notice problems, imperfections, or untidiness.
   _____ C. don't tend to notice or get bothered by clutter.

3. I prefer to make my living space . . .

_____ A. beautiful.

_____ B. organized.

_____ C. creative chaos.

4. When doing my job I like to . . .

_____ A. be passionate and energetic.

_____ B. make sure everything is accurate.

_____ C. consider future possibilities / wonder about the best way forward.

5. When talking to other people, I might come across as . . .

_____ A. affectionate.

_____ B. realistic.

_____ C. philosophical.

6. The disadvantage of my clothing style is that it may be . . .

_____ A. decadent.

_____ B. unimaginative.

_____ C. mismatched or uncoordinated.

7. In general, I carry myself . . .

_____ A. buoyantly.

_____ B. briskly.

_____ C. aimlessly.

8. My room is . . .

_____ A. richly decorated.

_____ B. neatly arranged.

_____ C. messy.

9. Generally, I tend to . . .

____ A. have a strong desire for things.
____ B. be critical but clear thinking.
____ C. be in my own world.

10. At school, I might have been known for . . .

____ A. having lots of friends.
____ B. being intellectual.
____ C. daydreaming.

11. I usually wear clothes in a way that is . . .

____ A. fashionable and attractive.
____ B. neat and orderly.
____ C. carefree.

12. I come across as . . .

____ A. affectionate.
____ B. thoughtful.
____ C. absentminded.

13. When other people are enthusiastic about something, I . . .

____ A. jump on board and want to get involved.
____ B. might be skeptical of it.
____ C. go off on tangents.

Now add up the numbers in each category (A, B, C) to get a crude score for each category. The category with the *lowest* score equals your greatest tendency. A = Faithful/Greedy, B = Discerning/Aversive, C = Speculative/Deluded.

Here are some general summaries for the categories:

A. Faithful/Greedy: You tend to be optimistic, affectionate and might even be popular. You are composed and quick thinking in everyday tasks. You are more likely to be attracted to sensual pleasure. You put faith into what you believe, and your passionate nature makes you popular with other people. You have a confident posture. At times you might become greedy for success. You crave pleasant experiences, good company, rich foods and can become proud. Your desire for superficial things sometimes leaves you discontented and at its worst may even lead you to manipulate others.

B. Discerning/Aversive: You tend to be clear thinking and discerning. Your intellect allows you to see things logically and identify flaws in things. You are quick to understand concepts, and tend to keep things organized and tidy while getting things done quickly. You pay attention to detail. You might even have a stiff posture. At times you are judgmental and critical. You might notice a strong dislike for certain people, places, or things. On a bad day, you may come across as grumpy or as a perfectionist.

C. Speculative/Deluded: You tend to be easygoing and tolerant. You are able to reflect on the future and speculate on what might happen. You think about things deeply and philosophically. You might have a posture that is uneven and variable. At times you might easily get caught up in your own thoughts or fantasies. As you daydream, sometimes you might become doubtful and worried about things. Lost in thought, you find yourself going along with what others suggest, perhaps even being easily persuaded. At your worst, you are disorganized, restless, and absentminded.

Notes

Introduction

1. E. L. Thorndike, "Animal Intelligence: An Experimental Study of the Associative Processes in Animals," *Psychological Monographs: General and Applied* 2, no. 4 (1898): 1–8.

2. B. F. Skinner, *The Behavior of Organisms: An Experimental Analysis* (New York: Appleton-Century, 1938).

3. J. Kabat-Zinn, *Full Catastrophe Living: Using the Wisdom of Your Body and Mind to Face Stress, Pain, and Illness,* rev. ed. (New York: Delacorte, 2013), xxxv.

4. S. Batchelor, *After Buddhism: Rethinking the Dharma for a Secular Age* (New Haven, Conn.: Yale University Press, 2015), 64.

5. Ibid., 23.

Chapter 1. Addiction, Straight Up

1. L. T. Kozlowski et al., "Comparing Tobacco Cigarette Dependence with Other Drug Dependencies: Greater or Equal 'Difficulty Quitting' and 'Urges to Use' but Less 'Pleasure' from Cigarettes," *JAMA* 261, no. 6 (1989): 898–901.

2. J. A. Brewer et al., "Mindfulness Training and Stress Reactivity in Substance Abuse: Results from a Randomized, Controlled Stage I Pilot Study," *Substance Abuse* 30, no. 4 (2009): 306–17.

3. J. D. Teasdale et al., "Prevention of Relapse/Recurrence in Major Depression by Mindfulness-Based Cognitive Therapy," *Journal of Consulting and Clinical Psychology* 68, no. 4 (2000): 615–23; J. Kabat-Zinn, L. Lipworth, and R. Burney, "The Clinical Use of Mindfulness Meditation for the Self-Regulation of Chronic Pain," *Journal of Behavioral Medicine* 8, no. 2 (1985): 163–90; J. Kabat-Zinn et al., "Effectiveness of a Meditation-Based Stress Reduction Program in the Treatment of Anxiety Disorders," *American Journal of Psychiatry* 149, no. 7 (1992): 936–43.

4. J. A. Brewer et al., "Mindfulness Training for Smoking Cessation: Results from a Randomized Controlled Trial," *Drug and Alcohol Dependence* 119, nos. 1–2 (2011): 72–80.

5. H. M. Elwafi et al., "Mindfulness Training for Smoking Cessation: Moderation of the Relationship between Craving and Cigarette Use," *Drug and Alcohol Dependence* 130, nos. 1–3 (2013): 222–29.

6. G. DeGraff, *Mind like Fire Unbound: An Image in the Early Buddhist Discourses,* 4th ed. (Valley Center, Calif.: Metta Forest Monastery, 1993).

7. B. Thanissaro, trans., *Dhammacakkappavattana Sutta: Setting the Wheel of Dhamma in Motion* (1993); available from Access to Insight: Readings in Theravada Buddhism, www.accesstoinsight.org/tipitaka/sn/sn56/sn56.011.than.html.

8. J. A. Brewer, H. M. Elwafi, and J. H. Davis, "Craving to Quit: Psychological Models and Neurobiological Mechanisms of Mindfulness Training as Treatment for Addictions," *Psychology of Addictive Behaviors* 27, no. 2 (2013): 366–79.

Chapter 2. Addicted to Technology

The chapter epigraph is from Nassim Nicholas Taleb, quoted in Olivier Goetgeluck's blog, https://oliviergoetgeluck.wordpress.com/the-bed-of-procrustes-nassim-nicholas-taleb.

1. C. Duhigg, *The Power of Habit: Why We Do What We Do in Life and Business* (New York: Random House, 2012); R. Hawkins et al., "A Cellular Mechanism of Classical Conditioning in *Aplysia:* Activity-Dependent Amplification of Presynaptic Facilitation." *Science* 219, no. 4583 (1983): 400–405.

2. B. F. Skinner, *Science and Human Behavior* (New York: Free Press, 1953), 73.

3. D. I. Tamir and J. P. Mitchell, "Disclosing Information about the Self Is Intrinsically Rewarding." *Proceedings of the National Academy of Sciences* 109, no. 21 (2012): 8038–43.

4. D. Meshi, C. Morawetz, and H. R. Heekeren, "Nucleus Accumbens Response to Gains in Reputation for the Self Relative to Gains for Others Predicts Social Media Use," *Frontiers in Human Neuroscience* 7 (2013).

5. L. E. Sherman et al., "The Power of the Like in Adolescence: Effects of Peer Influence on Neural and Behavioral Responses to Social Media," *Psychological Science* 27, no. 7 (2016): 1027–35.

6. R. J. Lee-Won, L. Herzog, and S. G. Park, "Hooked on Facebook: The Role of Social Anxiety and Need for Social Assurance in Problematic Use of Facebook," *Cyberpsychology, Behavior, and Social Networking* 18, no. 10 (2015): 567–74.

7. Z. W. Lee, C. M. Cheung, and D. R. Thadani, "An Investigation into the Problematic Use of Facebook," paper presented at the 45th Hawaii International Conference on System Science, 2012.

8. M. L. N. Steers, R. E. Wickham, and L. K. Acitelli, "Seeing Everyone Else's Highlight Reels: How Facebook Usage Is Linked to Depressive Symptoms," *Journal of Social and Clinical Psychology* 33, no. 8 (2014): 701–31.

9. U Pandita, *In This Very Life: The Liberation Teachings of the Buddha* (Somerville, Mass.: Wisdom Publications, 1992), 162.

Chapter 3. Addicted to Ourselves

The chapter epigraph is from Alan Watts, *This Is It, and Other Essays on Zen and Spiritual Experience* (New York: Vintage, 1973), 70.

1. J. A. Brewer et al., "Meditation Experience Is Associated with Differences in Default Mode Network Activity and Connectivity," *Proceedings of the National Academy of Sciences* 108, no. 50 (2011): 20254–59.

2. M. R. Leary, *The Curse of the Self: Self-Awareness, Egotism, and the Quality of Human Life* (Oxford: Oxford University Press, 2004), 18.

3. Watts, "This Is It," in *This Is It,* 70.

4. W. Schultz, "Behavioral Theories and the Neurophysiology of Reward," *Annual Review of Psychology* 57 (2006): 87–115.

5. W. J. Livesley, K. L. Jang, and P. A. Vernon, "Phenotypic and Genetic Structure of Traits Delineating Personality Disorder," *Archives of General Psychiatry* 55, no. 10 (1998): 941–48.

6. S. N. Ogata et al., "Childhood Sexual and Physical Abuse in Adult Patients with Borderline Personality Disorder," *American Journal of Psychiatry* 147, no. 8 (1990): 1008–13.

7. S. K. Fineberg et al., "A Computational Account of Borderline Personality Disorder: Impaired Predictive Learning about Self and Others through Bodily Simulation," *Frontiers in Psychiatry* 5 (2014): 111.

Chapter 4. Addicted to Distraction

The epigraph from Cornel West is taken from his *New York Times* editorial "Dr. King Weeps from His Grave," August 25, 2011, www.nytimes.com/2011/08/26/opinion/martin-luther-king-jr-would-want-a-revolution-not-a-memorial.html?_r=0. The epigraph from Sherry Turkle comes from an interview in the *Economic Times,* July 8, 2011, http://articles.economictimes.indiatimes.com/2011-07-08/news/29751810_1_social-networking-sherry-turkle-facebook/2.

1. B. Worthen, "The Perils of Texting while Parenting," *Wall Street Journal,* September 29, 2012, www.wsj.com/articles/SB10000872396390444772404577589683644202996.

2. C. Palsson, "That Smarts! Smartphones and Child Injuries," working paper, Department of Economics, Yale University, 2014.

3. J. L. Nasar and D. Troyer, "Pedestrian Injuries due to Mobile Phone Use in Public Places," *Accident Analysis and Prevention* 57 (2013): 91–95.

4. M. Horn, "Walking while Texting Can Be Deadly, Study Shows," *USA Today,* March 8, 2016, www.usatoday.com/story/news/2016/03/08/pedestrian-fatalities-surge-10-percent/81483294.

5. M. A. Killingsworth and D. T. Gilbert, "A Wandering Mind Is an Unhappy Mind," *Science* 330, no. 6006 (2010): 932.

6. J. A. Brewer, K. A. Garrison, and S. Whitfield-Gabrieli, "What about the 'Self' Is Processed in the Posterior Cingulate Cortex?," *Frontiers in Human Neuroscience* 7 (2013).

7. K. N. Ochsner and J. J. Gross, "The Cognitive Control of Emotion," *Trends in Cognitive Sciences* 9, no. 5 (2005): 242–49.

8. A. F. Arnsten, "Stress Signalling Pathways That Impair Prefrontal Cortex Structure and Function," *Nature Reviews Neuroscience* 10, no. 6 (2009): 410–22.

9. W. Hofmann et al., "Everyday Temptations: An Experience Sampling Study of Desire, Conflict, and Self-Control," *Journal of Personality and Social Psychology* 102, no. 6 (2011): 1318–35.

Chapter 5. Addicted to Thinking

The chapter epigraph comes from a compilation of Eckhart Tolle's observations on thinking, posted on YouTube: https://www.youtube.com/watch?v=YtKciyNpEs8.

1. In teaching hospitals, this has traditionally been considered a rite of passage or a mild hazing ritual disguised as teaching. Typically, a professor or resident physician questions a medical student, in front of the entire team of doctors and students, about her or his knowledge of a diagnosis or something else relevant to a patient that they have just seen on rounds. In theory, this questioning is aimed at testing (and disseminating) knowledge, though because the likelihood that the student knows as much as the professor is close to zero, it most often is stressful for the student, and ends in humiliation. In medical school, my friends and I would share war stories when we met up in the library or lunch: "What did you get pimped on today? Oh man, ouch."

2. K. Spain, "T-P in Beijing: Lolo Jones' Hopes of Gold Medal Clipped by Fall," *New Orleans Times-Picayune,* August 19, 2008, http://blog.nola.com/tpsports/2008/08/lolo_jones_hopes_of_gold_medal.html.

3. S. Gregory, "Lolo's No Choke," *Time,* July 19, 2012, http://olympics.time.com/2012/07/19/lolo-jones-olympic-hurdler.

4. S. Nolen-Hoeksema, B. E. Wisco, and S. Lyubomirsky, "Rethinking Rumination," *Perspectives on Psychological Science* 3, no. 5 (2008): 400–424.

5. R. N. Davis and S. Nolen-Hoeksema, "Cognitive Inflexibility among Ruminators and Nonruminators," *Cognitive Therapy and Research* 24, no. 6 (2000): 699–711.

6. Y. Millgram et al., "Sad as a Matter of Choice? Emotion-Regulation Goals in Depression," *Psychological Science* 2015: 1–13.

7. M. F. Mason et al., "Wandering Minds: The Default Network and Stimulus-Independent Thought," *Science* 315, no. 5810 (2007): 393–95.

8. D. H. Weissman et al., "The Neural Bases of Momentary Lapses in Attention," *Nature Neuroscience* 9, no. 7 (2006): 971–78.

9. D. A. Gusnard et al., "Medial Prefrontal Cortex and Self-Referential Mental Activity: Relation to a Default Mode of Brain Function," *Proceedings of the National Academy of Sciences* 98, no. 7 (2001): 4259–264.

10. S. Whitfield-Gabrieli et al., "Associations and Dissociations between Default and Self-Reference Networks in the Human Brain," *NeuroImage* 55, no. 1 (2011): 225–32.

11. J. A. Brewer et al., "Meditation Experience Is Associated with Differences in Default Mode Network Activity and Connectivity," *Proceedings of the National Academy of Sciences* 108, no. 50 (2011): 20254–59.

Chapter 6. Addicted to Love

1. A. Aron et al., "Reward, Motivation, and Emotion Systems Associated with Early-Stage Intense Romantic Love," *Journal of Neurophysiology* 94, no. 1 (2005): 327–37.

2. H. Fisher, "The Brain in Love," February 2008, TED, https://www.ted.com/talks/helen_fisher_studies_the_brain_in_love?language=en#t-159085. The poem begins at 2:51.

3. A. Bartels and S. Zeki, "The Neural Correlates of Maternal and Romantic Love," *NeuroImage* 21, no. 3 (2004): 1155–66.

4. K. A. Garrison et al., "BOLD Signal and Functional Connectivity Associated with Loving Kindness Meditation," *Brain and Behavior* 4, no. 3 (2014): 337–47.

Chapter 7. Why Is It So Hard to Concentrate—or Is It?

The quotation from Einstein used as an epigraph is from a letter to Carl Seelig, March 11, 1952.

1. J. D. Ireland, trans., *Dvayatanupassana Sutta: The Noble One's Happiness* (1995), available from Access to Insight: Readings in Theravada Buddhism, www.accesstoinsight.org/tipitaka/kn/snp/snp.3.12.irel.html.

2. *Magandiya Sutta: To Magandiya (MN 75)*, in *The Middle Length Discourses of the Buddha: A Translation of the Majjhima Nikāya,* trans. B. Ñāṇamoli and B. Bodhi (Boston: Wisdom Publications, 1995).

3. B. Bodhi, ed., *In the Buddha's Words: An Anthology of Discourses from the Pali Canon* (Somerville, Mass.: Wisdom Publications, 2005), 192–93.

4. G. Harrison, *In the Lap of the Buddha* (Boston: Shambhala, 2013).

5. Bodhi, *In the Buddha's Words.*

6. *Magandiya Sutta.*

7. B. F. Skinner and J. Hayes, *Walden Two* (New York: Macmillan, 1976 [1948]).

8. Hafiz, "And Applaud," from the Penguin publication *I Heard God Laughing: Poems of Hope and Joy,* trans. Daniel Ladinsky (New York: Penguin, 2006), 5. Copyright © 1996 and 2006 by Daniel Ladinsky and used with his permission.

9. *Anapanasati Sutta: Mindfulness of Breathing (MN 118)*. 2010.

10. Equanimity can be operationally defined as a mental calmness, composure, and evenness of temper, especially in a difficult situation.

11. M. Oliver, "Sometimes," in *Red Bird: Poems* (Boston: Beacon, 2008), 35.

Chapter 8. Learning to Be Mean—and Nice

The epigraph is from William H. Herndon and Jesse William Weik, *Herndon's Lincoln: The True Story of a Great Life,* vol. 3, chap. 14.

1. J. Mahler, "Who Spewed That Abuse? Anonymous Yik Yak App Isn't Telling," *New York Times,* March 8, 2015.

2. B. Ñāṇamoli and B. Bodhi, trans., *The Middle Length Discourses of the Buddha: A Translation of the Majjhima Nikāya* (Boston: Wisdom Publications, 1995).

3. J. Davis, "Acting Wide Awake: Attention and the Ethics of Emotion" (PhD diss., City University of New York, 2014).

4. H. A. Chapman et al., "In Bad Taste: Evidence for the Oral Origins of Moral Disgust," *Science* 323, no. 5918 (2009): 1222–26.

5. U. Kirk, J. Downar, and P. R. Montague, "Interoception Drives Increased Rational Decision-Making in Meditators Playing the Ultimatum Game," *Frontiers in Neuroscience* 5 (2011).

6. A. G. Sanfey et al., "The Neural Basis of Economic Decision-Making in the Ultimatum Game," *Science* 300, no. 5626 (2003): 1755–58.

7. S. Batchelor, *After Buddhism: Rethinking the Dharma for a Secular Age* (New Haven, Conn.: Yale University Press, 2015), 242.

8. T. Bhikkhu, "No Strings Attached," in *Head and Heart Together: Essays on the Buddhist Path* (2010), 12.

Chapter 9. On Flow

1. M. Csíkszentmihályi, *Beyond Boredom and Anxiety: Experiencing Flow in Work and Play* (San Francisco: Jossey-Bass, 1975).

2. M. Csíkszentmihályi, "Go with the Flow," interview by J. Geirland, *Wired,* September 1996, www.wired.com/1996/09/czik.

3. J. Nakamura and M. Csíkszentmihályi, "Flow Theory and Research," in *The Oxford Handbook of Positive Psychology,* 2nd ed., ed. S. J. Lopez and C. R. Snyder, 195–206 (New York: Oxford University Press, 2009).

4. D. Potter, "Dean Potter: The Modern Day Adventure Samurai," interview by Jimmy Chin, *Jimmy Chin's Blog,* May 12, 2014. "BASE" is an acronym for "building, antenna, span, earth."

5. P. Jackson and H. Delehanty, *Eleven Rings: The Soul of Success* (New York: Penguin, 2013), 23.

6. Sujiva, "Five Jhana Factors of Concentration/Absorption," 2012, BuddhaNet, www.buddhanet.net/mettab3.htm.

7. M. Csíkszentmihályi, *Finding Flow: The Psychology of Engagement with Everyday Life* (New York: Basic Books, 1997), 129.

8. C. J. Limb and A. R. Braun, "Neural Substrates of Spontaneous Musical Performance: An fMRI Study of Jazz Improvisation," *PLoS One* 3, no. 2 (2008): e1679; S. Liu et al., "Neural Correlates of Lyrical Improvisation: An fMRI Study of Freestyle Rap," *Scientific Reports* 2 (2012): 834; G. F. Donnay et al., "Neural Substrates of Interactive Musical Improvisation: An fMRI Study of 'Trading Fours' in Jazz," *PLoS One* 9, no. 2 (2014): e88665.

9. T. S. Eliot, "Burnt Norton," in *Four Quartets.* In the United States: excerpts from "Burnt Norton" from *Four Quartets* by T. S. Eliot. Copyright 1936 by Houghton Mifflin Harcourt Publishing Company; Copyright © renewed 1964 by T. S. Eliot. Reprinted by permission of Houghton Mifflin Harcourt Publishing Company. All rights reserved. In the UK and the rest of the world: published by Faber and Faber Ltd., reprinted with permission.

10. M. Steinfeld and J. Brewer, "The Psychological Benefits from Reconceptualizing Music-Making as Mindfulness Practice," *Medical Problems of Performing Artists* 30, no. 2 (2015): 84–89.

11. S. Kotler, *The Rise of Superman: Decoding the Science of Ultimate Human Performance* (Boston: New Harvest, 2014), 57.

Chapter 10. Training Resilience

The chapter epigraph comes from Andrew Boyd, *Daily Afflictions: The Agony of Being Connected to Everything in the Universe* (New York: Norton, 2002), 89.

1. Lao Tzu, *Tao Te Ching*, trans. Stephen Mitchell (New York: Harper Perennial, 1992), chap. 59.

2. S. Del Canale et al., "The Relationship between Physician Empathy and Disease Complications: An Empirical Study of Primary Care Physicians and Their Diabetic Patients in Parma, Italy," *Academic Medicine* 87, no. 9 (2012): 1243–49; D. P. Rakel et al., "Practitioner Empathy and the Duration of the Common Cold," *Family Medicine* 41, no. 7 (2009): 494–501.

3. M. S. Krasner et al., "Association of an Educational Program in Mindful Communication with Burnout, Empathy, and Attitudes among Primary Care Physicians," *JAMA* 302, no. 12 (2009): 1284–93.

4. T. Gyatso (Dalai Lama XIV), *The Compassionate Life* (Somerville, Mass.: Wisdom Publications, 2003), 21.

5. Krasner et al., "Educational Program in Mindful Communication."

6. The quotation was published in the *Bankers Magazine* in 1964 and has also been attributed to Will Rogers.

7. B. Thanissaro, trans., *Dhammacakkappavattana Sutta: Setting the Wheel of Dhamma in Motion* (1993); available from Access to Insight: Readings in Theravada Buddhism, www.accesstoinsight.org/tipitaka/sn/sn56/sn56.011.than.html.

8. S. Batchelor, *After Buddhism: Rethinking the Dharma for a Secular Age* (New Haven, Conn.: Yale University Press, 2015), 27; emphasis in the original.

9. Ibid., 125.

10. T. S. Eliot, "Little Gidding," in *Four Quartets*. In the United States: excerpts from "Little Gidding" from *Four Quartets* by T. S. Eliot. Copyright 1942 by T. S. Eliot; Copyright © renewed 1970 by Esme Valerie Eliot. Reprinted by permission of Houghton Mifflin Harcourt Publishing Company. All rights reserved. In the UK and the rest of the world: published by Faber and Faber Ltd., reprinted with permission.

Epilogue. The Future Is Now

1. A. D. Kramer, J. E. Guillory, and J. T. Hancock, "Experimental Evidence of Massive-Scale Emotional Contagion through Social Networks," *Proceedings of the National Academy of Sciences* 111, no. 24 (2014): 8788–90.

2. M. Moss, "The Extraordinary Science of Addictive Junk Food," *New York Times Magazine,* February 20, 2013.

3. S. Martino et al., "Informal Discussions in Substance Abuse Treatment Sessions," *Journal of Substance Abuse Treatment* 36, no. 4 (2009): 366–75.

4. K. M. Carroll et al., "Computer-Assisted Delivery of Cognitive-Behavioral Therapy for Addiction: A Randomized Trial of CBT4CBT," *American Journal of Psychiatry* 165, no. 7 (2008): 881–88.

Appendix. What Is Your Mindfulness Personality Type?

1. A. Buddhaghosa, *The Path of Purification: Visuddhimagga* (Kandy, Sri Lanka: Buddhist Publication Society, 1991).

2. N. T. Van Dam et al., "Development and Validation of the Behavioral Tendencies Questionnaire," *PLoS One* 10, no. 11 (2015): e0140867.

Acknowledgments

I'd like to offer a deep bow of gratitude all of the people who directly helped bring this book together whether editing, providing feedback or otherwise: Jennifer Banks, Katie Hall, Jerry Weinstein, Jon Kabat-Zinn, Mahri Leonard-Fleckman, Alice Brewer, Tracy George, Dianne Horgan, Catherine Krame, Nikhilesh Jha, and the team at Yale University Press.

I'm grateful for the teachers who have helped with my personal journey into mindfulness practices: Ginny Morgan, Joseph Goldstein, Thanissaro Bhikkhu, and the many teachers with whom I have sat retreat, or received guidance.

I'm grateful for my research and clinical teams and collaborators, past and present, who have contributed to our collective understanding of habit formation, and have helped move us toward alleviating suffering: Sarah Bowen, Willoughby Britton, Dan Brown, Kathy Carroll, Neha Chawla, John Churchill, Todd Constable, Jake Davis, Gaëlle Desbordes, Cameron Deleone, Susan Druker, Hani Elwafi, Kathleen Garrison, Jeremy Gray, Rick Hecht, Sean (Dae) Houlihan, Catherine Kerr, Hedy Kober, Sarah Mallik, G. Alan Marlatt, Ashley Mason, Linda Mayes, Cinque McFarlane-Blake, Candace Minnix-Cotton, Stephanie Noble, Stephanie O'Malley, Alex Ossadtchi, Prasanta Pal, Xenios Papademetris, Lori Pbert, Mark Pflieger, Marc Potenza, Maolin Qiu, Rahil Rojiani, Bruce Rounsaville, Andrea Ruf,

Juan Santoyo, Cliff Saron, Dustin Scheinost, Poppy Schoenberg, Rajita Sinha, Evan Thompson, Tommy Thornhill, Nicholas Van Dam, Remko van Lutterveld, Katie Witkiewitz, Jochen Weber, Sue Whitfield-Gabrieli, Patrick Worhunsky, Hua Yang.

I am also grateful for all of the individuals from whom I've learned so much in so many ways: Brett Ahlstrom, Eowyn Ahlstrom, Doug Alexander, Bhikkhu Analayo, Lee Barbera, Owen Becker, Emily Bleimund, Leigh Brasington, Allison Brewer, Bret Brewer, Kris Brewer, Jill Brockelman, Colleen Camenisch, Rodrigo Canales, Vincent Cangiano, Meg Chang, Si-lam Choy, Cathy Cukras, Rick Curtis, Lama Surya Das, Tim DeGavre, Brenda Fingold, Doran Fink, Philip Fleckman, Margaret Fletcher, Carl Fulwiler, Gawain Gilkey, Morgen Govindan, Sushant Govindan, Patrick Guilmot, Tarin Greco, Holly Haefele, Heidi Harbison, Dan Harris, Nick Halay, Charlie Hartwell, Austin Hearst, Nate Hellman, Gwenola Herbette, Patricia Holland, Fr. Michael Holleran, Andrew Hopper, Eugene Hsaio, Arianna Huffington, Charlie Hunter, Jeremy Hunter, Daniel Ingram, Bob Jacobson, Jewel, Rani Jha, Shailesh Jha, Maitland Jones Jr., Felix Jung, Taylor Kimberly, Katherine King, Phoebe Koch, Lynn Koerbel, Peter Kovac, Bill Krame, Scott Kriens, Star Leonard-Fleckman, Clayton Lightfoot, Coleman Lindsley, Colin Livesey, Lisa Lochner, Paulo Machado, Julian Marshall, Florence Meleo-Meyer, Aaron Miller, Trish Missall, Lisa Muglia, Lou Muglia, Kara Nance, Barnes Pederson, Virginia Pierce, Katie Prager, Bill Pugh, Heidi Rayala, Alicia Romeo, Josh Roman, Tim Ryan, Sharon Salzburg, Saki Santorelli, Pete Schwartz, Ron Serrano, Jill Shephard, Timmy Sullivan, Michael Taft, Victor van Berkel, Jeff Walker, Gary Weber and many more.

Index

INDEX

Johns Hopkins University, 201
Jones, Lori "Lolo," 95–96, 97, 178
Jones, Maitland, Jr., 93–94, 121
Jordan, Michael, 167
Joy: and concentration, 137–41; excitement vs., 141, 143–44; and flow, 168–69

Kabat-Zinn, Jon, ix, 12, 201; *Full Catastrophe Living,* xxiii, 126
Kahneman, Daniel, 87, 99
Kandel, Eric, 1
Kant, Immanuel, 155
Kerr, Cathy, 110
Killingsworth, Matt, 84, 85
Kirk, Ulrich, 156
Knee-jerk reactions, 7–8
Kornfield, Jack, 91
Kotler, Steven: *The Rise of Superman,* 164, 174
Kramer, Adam, 196
Krasner, Mick, 183

Learned associations, xii, 14
Leary, Mark: *The Curse of the Self,* 60
Lee, Zach, 53
Lee-Won, Roselyn, 52–53
Lincoln, Abraham, 148
Lombardi, Vince, 174
Louis C.K., 149–50, 154
Love, addiction to, 117–30; being in love vs. addiction to love, 125–30; chemical romance, 117–21; and PCC activation, 128–30; selfless love, 125–26, 183; winning the game of love, 121–25
"The Love Competition" (Stanford University), 117, 121–25

Loving-kindness, 102, 126–30, 183
Lutterveld, Remko van, 203

Mahler, Jonathan, 148, 149
Major Taylor Velodrome (Indianapolis), 162
Mallik, Sarah, 33
Marketing, 197–98
Marlatt, Alan, 25, 26
Martino, Steve, 200
Mason, Malia, 99, 101, 111
Maternal affection, 70
MBRP (Mindfulness-Based Relapse Prevention), 25–26
MBSR. *See* Mindfulness-Based Stress Reduction
McDonald, Michelle, 30
Medial prefrontal cortex, 87, 100, 103–4
Meditation: and concentration, 133–47; and flow, 167–68; and happiness, 134–37; and mind wandering, 102; and PCC activation, 103–16; process of, 91–92; smoking cessation study, 32–41; targeting of cravings through, 36–37
Memory, 1, 2, 39
Meshi, Dar, 48
Metta, 126–28
Mill, John Stuart, 155
Millgram, Yael, 98, 99
Mindfulness: addiction addressed with, 24–41; defined, 12–13; and empathy, 157; and learning, xii; as map, 13; process of, xvi–xvii, 11–14; self- addiction addressed with, 74–75; and subjective bias, 13, 14; surfing metaphor for, 24–28; training, 9–10

226